VISTA
THE CULTURE AND POLITICS OF GARDENS

VISTA

THE CULTURE AND POLITICS OF GARDENS

Edited by Noël Kingsbury and Tim Richardson

Frances Lincoln

Vista: The Culture and Politics of Gardens

Frances Lincoln Limited
4 Torriano Mews
Torriano Avenue
London NW5 2RZ
www.franceslincoln.com

First Frances Lincoln Edition: 2005

A catalogue record for this book is available from the British Library.

ISBN 07112 2575 3

Edited and designed by Kate Gallimore

Printed in Singapore

9 8 7 6 5 4 3 2 1

CONTENTS

Noël Kingsbury and Tim Richardson

Gardening. Most of us do it: mowing, watering, pruning, planting, weeding. What's it all about? Why do we garden? Why do we garden in the way we do? Why does our neighbour do something entirely different in their garden? Such questions are at the heart of explaining why we engage in any cultural activity. But is gardening or garden visiting a cultural activity like going to the ballet or theatre, or singing or reading? We argue that it is, although there may well be raised eyebrows in some quarters at such a description.

Like all cultural activities, there are reasons for why we do what we do, and why the neighbours do what they do. Explanations will inevitably involve discussing questions that are essentially philosophical or sociological in nature. In other words they will involve making a connection between gardening and the wider intellectual and cultural world. Once judgements come into play, as soon they must, then we stray into aesthetics and ethics, and from ethics into politics.

In most areas of cultural life these questions are raised routinely, but about gardening only rarely. In other words there is very little intellectual or critical discussion of gardens and gardening. *Vista* is intended to help redress this balance. But why should we bother? Apart from pleasing a few intellectuals who like something to discuss over their Sunday lunch, why should we be exploring these deeper questions? Surely gardening is simply a harmless hobby that gives pleasure to millions, and so long as we all live and let live there is no need to ask too many questions?

We want to ask questions for a variety of reasons. One is that we believe our gardens and our gardening will benefit as a result as nothing ever improves if no one questions it. Not only may our gardens, as pleasant, beautiful, inspiring places, be improved through some discussion, they may add another dimension entirely – that of being meaningful.

One of the most talked-about gardens of the last half century is Ian Hamilton Finlay's Little Sparta. This is not a garden of interesting plants, or clever design (although the views are impressive), but a garden that is about words, ideas and above all – meaning. The immense amount of interest that this garden has generated indicates perhaps that many of us are ready to explore gardens semiotically, to look at them as reflections of the world of ideas, words and meaning, of society, of culture and of politics.

Furthermore, gardening is not just about what we do on our own little patch, or in our window-boxes and hanging baskets. It is about gardens that are open to the public, about public parks, and with a little extension, about wherever we deliberately put plants for ornament, such as road embankments and the environs of the neighbourhood supermarket. These are all public places, the quality of which directly impinges on all of our lives, and yet all too often we are surrounded by ill-thought-out and degraded public landscapes. Bringing gardens and horticulture into the realm of intelligent public discourse and the ongoing debate over our relationship with our environment, will, we believe, con-tribute to a climate where we may see improvements.

So what is 'the culture and politics of gardens'? It was a delib-erately wide remit, and we have encouraged contributors to interpret it in their own ways – whether those be philosophical, political, aesthetic or horticultural. The result, we hope, is a stimulating, entertaining and diverse range of original essays that might appeal to anyone with a deeper interest in gardens than pure horticulture.

These essays are not united by a single theme: this first *Vista* is the opening salvo of what we hope might become an occasional publication devoted to airing ideas and theories about gardens which cannot find a place in the mainstream of commercial gar-den writing. Subsequent *Vistas* will be themed, but for this first one the brief was simply to consider gardens in their cultural context. What unites these sixteen essays is the way in which gardens are considered in a wider cultural context, not just as agglomerations of plants and hard materials. The intention has been to focus on the invisible meanings of gardens as much as their material reality.

Some of the essays are by writers already known to the gardening world, but some names will be new to readers. We have made a concerted effort to identify and encourage writers from different disciplines and backgrounds, in an attempt to transcend the traditionally insular and self-referential nature of garden writing. It is not in fact very difficult to be 'interdisciplinary' when it comes to gardens, because there is not really a 'discipline' of garden study. In the academic sphere, individuals with an interest in the subject might crop up in a wide range of faculties – landscape architecture, of course, but also art history, philosophy, geography, literature, environment, urban studies, psychology, anthropology, history, and so on. It is true that there are a number of MA courses in garden history and conservation in Britain, but their focus is on garden and landscape history – a subject we have tried to avoid in *Vista* as it is well catered for in other publications.

The reason we feel *Vista* is necessary now is because there seems to be a gulf between academic writing on gardens – which tends to be about history – and commercial writing on gardens, which focuses either on practical horticulture and plantsmanship, or on descriptions of individual gardens. There has been no single outlet for thinking on gardens that ranges wider than these parameters, and so when interesting new work with a gardens aspect is published, it tends to be secreted away in the specialist journals relating to other disciplines, where interested readers might not find it easily.

One motive for launching *Vista* is frankly hierarchical. For the past century or so the status of gardening and garden design in the hierarchy of the arts has been extremely low – and in Britain

the position has been shored up by a determinedly anti-intellectual streak among many influential gardeners and garden writers. This is a traditional British malaise, of course, but in the case
of gardens and gardening in the twentieth century it all but oblit-
erated any serious critical discourse. It is worth noting that this
was certainly not the case in the early eighteenth century, when
English landscape design was considered to be the cutting edge
of international avant-garde art and discussed as such by the
leading intellectuals of the day. The eighteenth century saw
Joseph Addison and Richard Payne Knight meditating deeply on
gardens, the twentieth century saw – well, we will refrain from
naming names. *Vista* is not going to change the gardens culture
overnight, or on its own, but we hope it might contribute to a
deeper appreciation of the place of gardens in our culture, and
help reveal the riches of the subject to those involved in other
disciplines who might otherwise have dismissed the subject as
unintellectual, irrelevant, old-fashioned, hobbyist, irredeemably
bourgeois or simply uncool.

Traditionally at this point in the introduction to a collection of
scholarly essays, the editors provide a brief rundown and sum-
mary of the ensuing articles. Since we have always tended to skip
these paragraphs ourselves, we thought we would omit them and
allow the essays to speak for themselves. There is a brief introduction to each, in any case.

We very much hope that *Vista* will be an occasional publication, encouraging debate on gardens and their place in society
and cultural life through future years. If you have any comments
on the contents of *Vista*, please contact us at reception@frances-
lincoln. com – subject matter 'Vista'.

Noël Kingsbury and Tim Richardson

GARDEN, ART, NATURE

David E. Cooper

In this essay, the author, a professor of philosophy, asks whether the appreciation of gardens is essentially a combination of two traditions – appreciation of nature, and of art – or whether their appeal is quite distinct.

Why, for millions of people, are gardens objects of serious appreciation and enjoyment? That's too large a question, of course, for a short essay or even a long tome, for a full answer would have to draw upon the contributions of psychology, history, sociology and much else. But there is a more manageable question, and one that first needs to be addressed if the larger one is to be tackled in an appropriate way: in what category should the kind of appreciation that gardens invite be located? Can it be assimilated to some already familiar kind, or is it more distinctive or unique?

Of course, this is still a large question, to which many answers have been offered. One thinks, for example, of the view, voiced by some 'deep ecologists', to the effect that people enjoy gardens for the same general reason they enjoy any manifestation of our 'conquest of nature', our controlling intervention in the natural world. But my discussion will focus on two more popular and less cynical answers, and, still more, on their combination into an especially familiar, even prevalent, answer.

The historian of gardens, John Dixon Hunt, indicates these two answers when he refers to the long debate, going back at least to 1700, 'between those who privileged art in the garden and those who saw it simply as nature'.[1] In one approach, the appreciation of gardens is to be assimilated to that of works of art; on the other, the assimilation is towards the enjoyment of nature. When, recalling remarks by Alexander Pope, Gertrude Jekyll describes herself as 'paint[ing] living pictures', or as 'painting a landscape with living things', she clearly invites us to experience her gardens somewhat as we do paintings.[2] Properly to enjoy a garden is to bring to bear upon it the modes of appreciation elicited by works of art. For Immanuel Kant, by contrast, the gardens that merit our appraisal – notably informal, 'English gardens' – are those which, though the products of artistry, are 'only beautiful … [because they] look like Nature'. In his view, we enjoy such gardens for the same reason we do scenes of untamed nature: they inspire the 'play' of our mental faculties, 'free from all constraints of arbitrary rules'.[3] Many later writers, while not subscribing to Kant's particular diagnosis of nature's appeal, have agreed with him in comparing the admiration of gardens with that of the natural, not the artefactual, world.

How should we judge these attempts to assimilate garden appreciation to art and to nature appreciation? No one would or should deny that, at certain moments or in certain moods, a person may be admiring a garden, or some part of it, on grounds similar to those that he or she has for admiring certain paintings or, perhaps, sculptures. Maybe it is the skilled composition of colours in a flowerbed, or what Mary Keen calls a 'balance between space and enclosures',[4] that strikes this admirer. Nor, equally, should one deny that, at other moments or in other moods, it is towards the natural, uncrafted beauty of certain flowers, or towards the mossy stones that have lain there for a thousand years, that the person's attention is drawn.

Such truisms, however, fall far short of conceding that garden appreciation is generally or typically akin either to art or to nature appreciation, that it must be assimilated to one or other of those aesthetic models. And there are good reasons for resisting each of those assimilations. To begin with, there are striking differences between the garden and the painting (or the sculpture) as objects of appreciation. I will mention just three. First, people admiring a garden are typically in, surrounded by, what they are admiring. Second, their experience is not normally of a discrete, framed object, for even a garden that is enclosed within high walls will usually owe its effect to the 'borrowing' of elements outside of the enclosure – distant hills, the sky, the sound of nearby cattle, or whatever. Third, enjoyment of a garden typically engages several, sometimes all, of the perceptual senses: we see the colours of the flowers, smell their perfume, hear them rustling in the breeze, even feel the textures on our fingers. By contrast, a painting is set before the spectator, an object contained in a frame, which engages vision alone among the senses.[5]

Pointing to these differences in effect reminds us of ways in which gardens are more akin to natural places than to *objets d'art*. But it would be a mistake to then assimilate garden appreciation to that of nature. Kant, recall, held that gardens are only beautiful when they 'look like Nature', but even in the case of 'English' gardens we are rarely unaware that these are gardens, and not wild or uncultivated places. If it is nature at all that we appreciate in such cases, this is 'nature-as-affected-by-humanity'.[6] By contrast, it is usually integral to the enjoyment of raw, wild nature that it is not 'affected-by-humanity'. That is why the lover of nature is liable to be disappointed, his enjoyment eroded, on discovering that what he took to be a natural scene is a 'fake', the product of artefact and not natural processes.

This consideration in effect reminds us of ways in which gardens are more akin to works of art than to nature. That reminder, taken together with the earlier and opposite reminder of ways in which gardens are closer to natural places than to works of art, makes it tempting to go for a compromise – to fuse together, while at the same time moderating, the two attempts at assimilation. Garden appreciation, so the idea goes, factors out into two kinds of appreciation – of art and of nature. This idea has proved sufficiently appealing to now be called the standard view. To take one example, more or less at random, the pioneering American writer on landscape design, A. J. Downing, held that the enjoyment of the best gardens is due both to the 'charm and polish' that 'art can bestow' – hence to the 'recognition of art' at work – and to the 'power', often 'rude and irregular', manifested by uncultivated nature.[7]

Tempting and even commonsensical as this compromise – this 'factorizing' approach, as I've called it elsewhere[8] – may sound, ultimately it is not compelling. (The grain of truth in it, to recall the truisms mentioned a few paragraphs earlier, is that someone's admiration, when in the garden, may, on occasion, be focused on some piece of gardener's artistry and, on other occasions, on some natural features that might also be found outside the precincts of the garden.) Let us start by noting an important implication, germane to the question I set out to address, that this compromise view has. What the view entails is that there is nothing genuinely distinctive or special about garden appreciation, for this turns out to be a compound of two other forms of appreciation. The garden appreciator merely brings to bear upon certain objects – gardens – two already established modes of appreciation, and then, as it were, adds them together. He or she is rather in the position of a judge of an Olympic diving event who assesses the divers' performances by estimating first their technical prowess and then their style, and then combines the estimates to determine the final scores.

Admirers of gardens, it seems to me, should be disturbed by this implication, for not only does it confound an intuitive conviction that there is something genuinely distinctive about garden appreciation, it is an implication that has often encouraged a deprecatory, even hostile, attitude towards gardens that purport to offer more than 'cheerful surroundings' and 'the pleasure of strolling'. Those words are Hegel's, who goes on to argue that gardens, as nature-plus-art, fail to be one thing or the other: they are unsuccessful as art, which should be an emphatically and exclusively human product, while also lacking in the 'greatness and freedom' of nature.[9] Hegel has had many followers in this attitude, not least among the deep ecologists referred to earlier.

It is, of course, one thing for a view to be disturbing to certain people, another for it to be actually mistaken. Nevertheless there are, I suggest, good reasons for rejecting the compromise or factorizing view of garden appreciation. I begin with a historical point. Tempting as it may seem to treat garden appreciation as a function, in part, of nature appreciation, this is hard to justify historically. In the West, as in Persia and Arabia – even, perhaps, in China – a tradition of appreciating gardens and other highly cultivated places, like orchards and oases, pre-dates one of valuing raw, wild nature. In Persian and Arabic poetry, for example, there were countless dithyrambs to gardens, but it is in the writings of Western travellers that one first encounters, on any scale, an aesthetic sensibility to what one such traveller called 'the eternal, irremediable sterility' of the desert.[10] As for Europe, there is ample evidence that appreciation of wilder natural places was, in its early phases at least, modelled on an already established tradition of garden appreciation – as well as, one should add, on traditions of artistic depictions of nature.[11] It would, therefore, be no less plausible to analyse or factorize the enjoyment of nature into, among other things, the enjoyment of gardens than vice versa.

The main objection to the factorizing approach, however, is of what might be called a phenomenological kind: the approach is unfaithful, and necessarily so, to our typical experience of gardens. The objection is best grasped by first considering what is, surely, a fairly obvious feature of such experience. While I conceded that the attention of the garden admirer might now be upon a piece of artistry in the garden (a colour drift, say), now upon some natural item (that gnarled old tree, perhaps), this is not the typical manner of attention. When I enter a garden and am struck by it, I do not find my attention oscillating between bits of artistry and bits of untouched nature. My experience is, one might say, more holistic, and it takes some effort on my part to admire a piece of topiary, for example, in isolation from the whole. This effort contrasts with the effortless appreciation I extend to the garden as I stroll around it, open to its total effect and sensitive to a range of effects that I am not in the business of breaking down into component ingredients.

But, you might ask, isn't the total effect nevertheless due to such components, ones on which I can, albeit with some effort, individually focus? The reply to this question takes us to the crux of the matter, to the phenomenological point I announced in the previous paragraph. Appreciation of the garden cannot be reduced to appreciation of these components, natural or artefactual, since it is only as components of a larger whole that they can be properly appreciated – can, indeed, be singled out and identified as significant components of the garden. Compare the claim that enjoyment of a piece of music is reducible to enjoyment of the phrases that compose it. What is wrong with this claim, among other things, is that it is only as being parts of the whole piece that these phrases are significant, that indeed they are phrases at all. The same sequence of notes occurring in another piece might not even constitute a musical phrase.

Let me illustrate the point I am driving at. Suppose I notice a particular drift of flowers in a bed, and duly record my admiration for the garden designer's artistry. Now the very same collection of flowers placed differently in another garden might not have attracted my notice and admiration at all: indeed, it might not constitute a drift at all, but instead be part of a larger one or a sequence of smaller ones punctuated as they are, let's suppose, by a number of urns. As another illustration, consider the following remarks by Roger Scruton: 'A tree in a garden is not like a tree in a forest ... It is not simply there ... accidental. It stands and watches ... converses in a sense, with those who walk beneath it and with other components of the garden, like the wall opposite or the bird-table at its side.'[12] His point is that the tree-in-the-garden is not typically experienced in the way that an identical tree-in-the-forest is, for it is the experience of the former that, for example, it towers above the lawn or that it is between the terrace and the summer-house. It is integral to the experience of the tree-in-the-garden, more generally, that, as Scruton puts it, the tree gathers about it other features of the garden.

My claim, then, is that it is not so much unusual as impossible for a person's appreciation or experience of a garden to consist in, or factor out into, that of independent components, artefactual and natural. For while one may indeed, with suitable effort, focus on such components separately and in succession, these are only the components they are – only the objects of experience they are – in virtue of their belonging to that very garden. If this is right, then the compromise view, according to which garden appreciation is to be understood as art-plus-nature appreciation, must be abandoned. The further implication is that we should take seriously the idea that appreciation of gardens is indeed distinctive and of its own kind, and not the result, therefore, of welding together the modes of appreciation suited to art objects and natural things respectively. If the garden is nature-as-affected-by-humanity, the hyphens need to be kept in, for the garden is a whole that cannot be dissolved into nature and human artistry. The challenge for the aesthetics of the garden – one that I cannot take up in this essay – is to illuminate the distinctive appeal of gardens, to understand what it is to appreciate a garden as a garden and not as something it isn't.[13]

NOTES

1. J. D. Hunt, 'Gardens: Historical Overview' in M. Kelly (ed.), *Encyclopedia of Aesthetics*, vol. 2, New York, 1998, pp. 272–3.

2. E. Lawrence (ed.), *The Gardener's Essential Gertrude Jekyll*, London, 1991, pp. 24, 160.

3. Immanuel Kant, *The Critique of Judgement*, 1914; trans. James Creed Meredith, Oxford, 1952, pp. 45 and 48.

4. Mary Keen, 'Gardens as Theatre' in E. Hunningher (ed.), *Gardens of Inspiration*, London, 2001, p. 112.

5. On these and other salient differences between gardens and paintings see Mara Miller, *The Garden as Art*, Albany, 1993.

6. M. Budd, *The Aesthetic Appreciation of Nature: Essays on the Aesthetics of Nature*, Oxford, 2002, p. 7. (My hyphens.)

7. A. J. Downing, *Landscape Gardening and Rural Architecture*, New York, 1991, pp. 51ff.

8. D. E. Cooper, 'In Praise of Gardens', *British Journal of Aesthetics*, 2003, 43, 2.

9. G. W. F. Hegel, *Aesthetics: Lectures on Fine Art*; trans. T. M. Knox, Oxford, 1975, pp. 699–700.

10. Norman Douglas, quoted by Yi-Fu Tuan, 'Desert and Ice: ambivalent aesthetics', in S. Kemal and I. Gaskell (eds), *Landscape, Natural Beauty and the Arts*, Cambridge, 1993, p. 145.

11. See K. Thomas, *Man and the Natural World: Changing Attitudes in England 1500–1800*, Harmondsworth, 1984.

12. R. Scruton, *Perictione in Colophon*, South Bend, Indiana, 2000.

13. I do take up this challenge, however, in my *A Philosophy of Gardens*, Oxford, forthcoming 2006.

THE GARDEN AS ART

George Carter

Why is garden writing dominated by horticultural concerns? This essay traces the evolution of thinking about gardens since the nineteenth century, and explains how and why the garden became segregated from the pantheon of the fine arts.

In the seventeenth, eighteenth and, to some extent, the nineteenth centuries, writing on gardens and gardening was as important to cultural and intellectual life as writing on the fine arts and architecture, and indeed related closely to them. This reflected the high cultural status of the art of the garden. Gardening was a sphere of activity not just related to horticulture, as it mainly is today, but one where thoughts on the aesthetics of landscape appreciation, the creation of elaborate symbolic schemes, views on architecture and sculpture, hydraulic engineering, scientific exploration, and a knowledge of ancient and modern world culture, all came into play to create an incredibly richly layered art that makes today's gardens seem impoverished.

If one looks at just one area – writing on the aesthetics of garden design – one finds that the shifting points of view were of great interest to a large readership. The nuances of the changing view of gardens in relation to nature in the eighteenth century, for instance, were plotted by the foremost writers of the day – Addison, Pope, Walpole, Mason, Gilpin, Price, Knight, to take a small random sample – who did not write narrowly on the subject, but were wide-ranging and discursive. They wrote about gardening seen against the broad spectrum of all the arts. In some ways gardens were at the very forefront in changes of taste because they were seen to relate to, and were the actual testing ground for, such important issues as the attitude to landscape, and to nature in the broadest sense. Why and when this attitude to garden writing changed is the subject of this essay. Whether it can be revitalized is the question it poses.

At the end of the nineteenth and the beginning of the twentieth centuries, the debate was still lively, though the cultural status of gardens had to some extent been eroded. A closer look at the controversy between the exponent of architectural gardens (Reginald Blomfield) and the anti-aesthetic 'nature-never-makes-a-mistake' view (William Robinson) indicates the direction writing on gardens was to move in the twentieth century. William Robinson's essay 'Garden Design and Architect's Gardens', published in July 1892, was a response to Blomfields's *The Formal Garden in England*, published in January of that year (with illustrations and research by H. Inigo Thomas). Blomfield, a successful architect favouring a rather literal Queen Anne style, took the Arts and Crafts view propounded by William Morris, that the garden 'should by no means imitate the wilfulness or wildness of nature but should look like a thing never seen except near a house'. On the other hand, Robinson, who rose from a position as a professional gardener to become one of the most prolific garden journalists and authors of the later nineteenth century, took nature as his cue and was anti-aesthetic to a degree. His attitude is encapsulated in this late (1913) comment on colour in the garden: 'Colour schemes: there is some talk of these nowadays. They need never be thought of if we take good care to have good plants which grow in natural forms...in the garden the most beautiful colour can be got by natural ways.' By October 1892 Blomfield was able to publish a riposte to Robinson in the second edition of his bestseller. He devoted twenty-one pages of his new preface to a minute dissection and demolition of Robinson's argument, a typical comment being:

'Mr Robinson does not understand the artistic importance of mass on the one hand, and scale on the other.'

Robinson was modern in the sense that he took his cue from the plants themselves rather than from a creative impetus to combine plants, architecture and a view of landscape using a highly developed aesthetic code. However, Robinson, by modern standards, is a highly educated writer and is interested in presenting his view of 'naturalism' against Blomfield's more historicist and aesthetic position. His gardening at least has a philosophy behind it.

Gertrude Jekyll, too, coming from an Arts and Crafts Movement background, writes cogently about both the physical process of gardening (she is the first generation of garden writer to be actively involved herself in gardening – digging, sowing, weeding and so on), and the aesthetics of it. From her fine art background she applied her views on colour and form – derived from painting – directly to planting. She also liberally sprinkled her writing with her wide-ranging knowledge of architecture, the history of furniture and craft, and brought a Modernist 'truth to materials' gloss to the subject of garden design. The success of her garden writing is due to her well-rounded view of the subject – again, richly layered with knowledge and inventive in its approach. However, her emphasis on the do-it-yourself aspect of gardening had an unfortunate effect on the garden journalism that was burgeoning in the early years of the twentieth century, to the extent that it has now developed almost entirely in the horticultural direction.

A distinct change in the status of gardens came with Modernism – a movement that addressed architecture and art decades before it took a line on garden design. Early Modernist architects were unsure as to what was an appropriate setting for rationalist buildings, and a wide range of approaches were adopted. Some – Le Corbusier among them – showed buildings dropped, as it were, into eighteenth-century-style informal landscape parks, or unadorned agricultural settings. Others, such as the Viennese architects Josef Hofmann and Adolf Loos, adopted a more formal rationalist approach to the setting of a building – an attitude taken to its most extreme form in Robert Mallet-Stevens's French-style abstract and geometric use of topiary. In fact, different exponents of Modernism were taking diametrically opposite views on basic questions. Was 'naturalism', or something more honestly artificial, the proper adjunct to a Modernist edifice? This has always been a problem with the Modernist garden – it never had a clearly defined philosophy. To the hard-line Modernist, the proper line to have taken would have been that history should be totally eschewed and that new ways of looking at the raw materials of gardens – plants and hard-landscaping – should be invented on a rational basis. One would necessarily need to be well-informed to disentangle and distance oneself from one's historically acquired response to nature and the landscape. Having myself been through an art school foundation course in the 1960s whose sole aim was to unlearn acquired responses and to shed visual clichés, I know how difficult, if not impossible, a process this is. The problem was that few exponents were aware of the historical nature of all their responses, and therefore they found it hard to shed them. What resulted was a divergent mishmash of styles.

One of the first writers to see that Modernism, not at all noted for its flexibility, lacked a clear line on garden design was Christopher Tunnard, author of *Gardens in the Modern Landscape*, published in 1938. He provided an astute survey of early Modernist attitudes to garden and landscape settings. One of the delightfully comic anomalies he draws attention to is a Behrens house in Northamptonshire set in a Jekyll/Lutyens vernacular garden. This is contrasted against more sophisticated continental examples of simple rationalist planting – asymmetrical formality that accorded well with early Modernist buildings. Tunnard was as fully aware of contemporary movements in painting and

sculpture as he was knowledgeable about the history of gardening and architecture. So he could see the point, for instance, of a
Picturesquely planned modern house at St Anne's Hill, Chertsey,
Surrey, built at the centre of an eighteenth-century Picturesquely
planned park. He was able to see that the late eighteenth-century
attitude to Picturesque asymmetrical planning in architecture
was closely related to the Modernist aesthetic based on bold
asymmetrical massing of volumes and voids.

The trouble with Modernism up until the 1970s was that it
was exclusive, po-faced, and had its back firmly set against history. This necessarily reduced the references that could be made:
form followed function in a sterile way that ignored all the
delightful richness locked away in the history of gardening and
architecture and in the individual history of plants themselves –
material which forms a rich seam to be mined by designers.

Charles Jencks, who defined the concept of Post-Modernism
in architecture,[1] tried to redress the balance by suggesting that
both architecture and gardens could be enriched by no longer
avoiding ornament but by linking it to meaningful symbolism –
positively encouraging an outburst of riotous and amusing ornamental detail. His own house and garden were used as a test case
and were extensively written about in *Towards a Symbolic
Architecture*.[2] Subsequently, his Scottish garden has taken the idea
further with the links it makes between garden design and current scientific and mathematical research.

For a long time the fine arts, and particularly the production
of site-related sculpture, was conducted in contexts that one
might have thought definitely engaged with gardens – but for
many years, the links between the two were hardly perceived
and there seemed, oddly, to be a great chasm dividing them.
Perhaps there was a high-handed approach on both sides: artists
unable to make a connection between the act of gardening and
their ad hoc view of intervention in landscapes; gardeners set
against anything that might downgrade plantsmanship as the

prime element of garden design. Gardening was certainly rather looked down on in the later twentieth century as a not-very-sophisticated offshoot of Modernist architecture at best, and a horticulture-led development of the Jekyll tradition at worst.

The fine arts have greatly enriched garden design. One thinks of the effect of abstract painting on the likes of Roberto Burle Marx or Luis Barragan in the 1940s and 1950s. However, in the last twenty or so years, the fine arts have been responsible for some radical shifts in our present-day view of what constitutes a garden. Many strands have come together to effect this, but sculpture has been particularly important. I am not so much here thinking of the public sculpture park – individual works set in a landscape – but those works that have interacted with their setting to such an extent that they create an entirely new one, or a new perception of what is possible or what is pleasing. I am thinking of the work of, for instance, Christo, who engages with a whole raft of issues in his large-scale temporary landscape installations, including public relations, aesthetics and politics. In another direction, Andy Goldsworthy's work using the raw materials of nature to create ephemeral works that reveal the fragility and impermanence of landscape have made us look at aspects of gardens that might previously have been cleared away: dead leaves, ice, mud, rotting foliage, and so on. Donald Judd's cool outdoor installations of concrete present that delightful age-old contrast of ordered geometry set against wilful nature.

There are many other examples, but perhaps one of the most useful catalysts in this country, in terms of space being made available for experimentation, was the National Garden Festival movement that ran during the 1980s. This created large-scale projects for collaboration between artists and landscape archi-tects in a fairly free-ranging, almost funfair atmosphere. I remember in particular two projects I worked on with Raf Fulcher: the outdoor amphitheatre at Stoke-on-Trent in 1985, and the central space at Glasgow in 1990. They both became flights of fancy that would be hard to envisage in any other context, unless it were the eighteenth-century London pleasure grounds of Vauxhall or Ranelagh.

My own *beau ideal* of garden design now would be an activity that incorporated and utilized many arts. It would be richly textured with meaning, perhaps – like Ian Hamilton Finlay's Little Sparta, or Gabriele d'Annunzio's Il Vittoriale – containing texts, inscriptions and messages, some obvious, some waiting to be decoded. It would have a strongly architectural element, with all the references that architecture brings. There would be a bold and dynamic sculptural element in the handling of the volumes and voids created by both the architecture and the planting. The planting itself would be chosen both for visual aesthetic reasons, for scent and for the associations that all plants conjure up – whether they be historical, geographical or seasonal. There would also be the lessons that painting brings: the use of colour, the contrast of texture and so on. Then there would be fun, humour and jokes contrasted against more serious aspects. There would be the possibilities of illusionism. There would be space dedicated to individual pieces of sculpture or ornament. Finally, there would be that contrast between complexity and simplicity, between jewel-like richness and large expanse of plain grass, or plain hedge, or sky that gives a garden pace and interest. Perhaps this sounds too rich a diet, but it is a synthesis that I have been attempting to recreate over the past twenty-five years, taking inspiration from the multi-layered, and I think more interesting, gardens of the seventeenth and eighteenth centuries.

Of course gardens now encompass a much wider spectrum of concerns than those listed above, which happen to reflect my own concerns. There is the question of sustainability; the position of gardens as part of the eco-system; the pros and cons of using native or introduced plants and the impact that that has on habitat. Those who write on gardens today need to have a very wide-ranging viewpoint – and to be fair, many do. It is not enough to be knowledgeable in one area only. The best writers of the last century had this broad approach: Vita Sackville-West, Russell Page, Sylvia Crowe, Geoffrey Jellicoe. It would be good if garden writing in the twenty-first century strayed into other fields: art criticism, the idea of nature, the relationship between gardening and agriculture, or the relationship between private and public gardens – to name but a few random subjects.

Since gardening is the one area where the individual has direct control of his or her own environment, and is at the same time Britain's most popular leisure pursuit, the potential for stimulating garden writing is great and the audience substantial. Let us hope that *Vista* helps to re-establish garden writing in the position it occupied in the past.

NOTES

1. Charles Jencks, *The Language of Post-Modern Architecture*, London, 1977.

2. Charles Jencks, *Towards a Symbolic Architecture*, New York, 1985.

THE GARDEN AND THE DIVISION OF LABOUR

Martin Hoyles

Garden history routinely attributes the design and making of gardens to the owners of the land. Everyone knows that gardens are really made by the workers employed by the landowner, but this truth is rarely acknowledged. This essay attempts to redress the balance.

> Who built Thebes, with its seven gates?
> In books we find the names of kings.
> Did the kings drag along the lumps of rock?
> And Babylon, many times destroyed –
> Who rebuilt it so many times?
> Where did the builders of glittering Lima live?
> On the evening, when the Chinese Wall was finished,
> Where did the masons go?
>> Bertolt Brecht, 'A Worker Questions History'
>> (1935)

Brecht might well have been thinking of the Hanging Gardens of Babylon, one of the Seven Wonders of the World, which were situated in what is now Iraq. It is said that they were 'built' by Nebuchadnezzar in the sixth century B.C. The gardens were made up of a series of huge terraces and galleries constructed on a hillside, supported by arches up to 170 feet high, with walls 22 feet thick. Water was drawn up from the River Euphrates to the top of the gardens and then channelled through conduits. Clearly it was a monumental task of manual labour.

MANUAL LABOUR

> You look in your history-books to see who built Westminster Abbey, who built St Sophia at Constantinople, and they tell you Henry III, Justinian the Emperor. Did they? Or, rather, men like you and me, handicraftsmen, who have left no names behind them, nothing but their work?
>
> William Morris, *The Lesser Arts* (1878)

There is a world of difference between the noun 'garden' and the verb 'gardening'. Most books on history and design concentrate on the 'garden' and usually leave out any mention of the hard labour of 'gardening'. The final product is analysed without reference to the division of labour, and this can be seen to correspond with the traditional class system: aristocratic ownership of the land, middle-class intellectual design, and working-class labour. Garden history has usually been a study of ownership, design and style; in other words, a story of gardens rather than gardening. Yet the labour in making gardens is crucial.

The attempt to hide the exploitation and division of labour involved in gardening is most apparent in the second half of the eighteenth century, the heyday of the English landscape garden. At this time 400 families owned a quarter of the cultivated land in England. The landscape garden, which was created in this period, is often seen as the greatest artistic invention of the English, and the credit for this is usually attributed to the designers: William Kent, 'Capability' Brown and Humphry Repton; or to the owners: the Duke of Devonshire at Chatsworth, the Duke of Marlborough at Blenheim, Viscount Cobham at Stowe.

When you consider the work involved, it is clear that most of the credit lies elsewhere. The landowners made the decisions, the designers made the plans, but the workers made the gardens. Landscapes had to be dug and dammed, planted and pruned.

In creating these landscape gardens whole villages might be destroyed to create pleasing vistas. In 1761, for example, Lord

Harcourt, at Nuneham near Oxford, created the 'deserted village' of Oliver Goldsmith's poem. The village street became a path in the park for viewing the valley below. The church was turned into a classical temple and the congregation, still responsible for its upkeep, now had to walk a mile and a half to worship. Cows were provided with a special underground passage so they could pass from field to field without spoiling the view.

The eighteenth-century English poet William Cowper calls 'Capability' Brown, who was the main architect of these landscape upheavals, an 'omnipotent magician' and in 'The Task' (1785) ironically catalogues his tricks:

> He speaks. The lake in front becomes a lawn,
> Woods vanish, hills subside, and vallies rise,
> And streams as if created for his use,
> Pursue the track of his directing wand
> Sinuous or strait, now rapid and now slow,
> Now murm'ring soft, now roaring in cascades,
> Ev'n as he bids.

'Capability' Brown gave the orders, but labourers did the work, and the workers who carried out these transformations are only occasionally remembered. In 1786 Thomas Jefferson, later to become president of the United States, visited England and toured some of the famous landscape gardens in order to 'estimate the expense of making and maintaining a garden in that style'. At Stowe he found 'fifteen men and eighteen boys employed in keeping the pleasure grounds'; and he notes of Blenheim's 2,500 acres: 'Two hundred people employed to keep it in order, and to make alterations and additions. About fifty of these employed in pleasure grounds.'

One of the hardest tasks in the garden was cutting the grass. Great care had to be taken to make the lawns look perfect. It would take three men with scythes a whole day to cut an acre of grass. They would be followed by lawn women who gathered up the grass cuttings. In 1721 at Canons Park in Middlesex, home of the Duke of Chandos, the grass was scythed two or three times a week and weeded every day. The lawns were often rolled and, according to the anonymous author of *The Gardener's New Kalendar* of 1758, 'care must be taken that the horses should be without shoes and have their feet covered with woollen mufflers'.

Well after the invention of the lawnmower in 1830, the hard work of scything lawns often continued, especially where there were many trees or flower-beds and the use of a mowing machine drawn by a horse was impractical. Scything was a skilled job, for the gardener had to keep the edge of the scythe at a uniform height throughout the whole length of the sweep. Gathering up the cuttings also had to be carried out meticulously, as any portion of cut grass left to wither would obstruct the edge of the scythe at the next mowing.

Another back-breaking task, carried out largely by women, was weeding. The earliest English records of women working as paid labourers in a garden are the entries in the fourteenth-century rolls of Ely Cathedral where women appear in the wages list for digging the vines and weeding. The number of historical references to weeding women is remarkable, and in the fourteenth century they were paid two-pence halfpenny a day, just half the male gardener's wage.

In 1516 women were paid three pence a day for removing charlock, nettles, convolvulus, dodder, thistles, dandelions and groundsel from the gardens at Hampton Court. In 1696 the accounts for the Royal Gardens at Hampton Court show that the labour force consisted of about sixty men paid by the year. In addition there were ten casual men whose daily rate was about two shillings. Women on casual rates were paid a third of this sum. In the nineteenth century, whilst a casual gardener would earn about five or six shillings a day, his weeding women helpers would only get paid about a sixth as much.

In 1644 John Evelyn, the famous English diarist, visited the Luxembourg Palace in Paris and he describes in his diary (1 April) the 'beautiful and magnificent' gardens, full of 'persons of quality, citizens and strangers, who frequent it, and to whom all access is freely permitted, so that you shall see some walks and retirements full of gallants and ladies; in others, melancholy friars; in others, studious scholars; in others, jolly citizens, some sitting or lying on the grass, others running and jumping; some playing bowls, others dancing and singing'. He ends with this significant note: 'What is most admirable, you see no gardeners, or men at work, and yet all is kept in such exquisite order, as if they did nothing else but work; it is so early in the morning, that all is despatched and done without the least confusion.'

The invisibility of workers was to be a particular ambition of owners of eighteenth-century landscape gardens. But already in the seventeenth century, as James Turner shows in *The Politics of Landscape*, poets generally leave out any reference to the violent labours of the countryside:

> It takes some effort to appreciate what has been censored from the ideal landscape. There is virtually no mention of land-clearance, tree-felling, pruning, chopping, digging, hoeing, weeding, branding, gelding, slaughtering, salting, tanning, brewing, boiling, smelting, forging, milling, thatching, fencing and hurdle-making, hedging, road-mending and haulage. Almost everything which anybody does in the countryside is taboo.[1]

Vistas of lawn, lake and trees could be seen from the big house or from other vantage points, but the labour on the land, which created the wealth to construct the vistas, was banished from sight. 'Capability' Brown had the flower, fruit and kitchen gardens hidden behind walled enclosures. The only human being you might see would be a hermit, specially hired to live in the hermitage (note the celebrated case of the Painshill hermit), and liable to be sacked if he did not live a sufficiently austere life.

Meanwhile, offstage, the hard work would go on, separating production from consumption. The enclosed fields were set out in mathematical grids with straight hedges and straight roads, in contrast to the winding curves of the landscape garden. The former were being organized for efficient capitalist farming, using new mechanical inventions such as Jethro Tull's seed drill, scientific crop rotation, and improved sheep and cattle breeding. This was the practical, productive side of the country estate. The garden, on the other hand, was the aesthetic side: the composed yet natural landscape of 'pleasing prospects' where sensibility could be cultivated.

PAY AND CONDITIONS

There is no class of gentlemen's servants so badly lodged as gardeners generally are.
John Loudon, *Encyclopaedia of Gardening* (1822)

In the winter, during periods of frost and snow, many gardeners would be laid off. In the nineteenth century, groups of them could be found begging in the streets, holding aloft the tools of their trade. The precarious nature of the job of gardening is illustrated in the employment practice at the famous Chelsea Physic Garden in London. In the diary of William Anderson, who was curator in 1815, dismissals are recorded and the reasons given: 'John Hutchins, discharged for a dunce', Henry Wood, 'too wise', another man 'for a blockhead'. Other gardeners were sacked for pilfering, fighting or getting drunk.

Many gardeners were made unemployed because of the invention of the lawnmower. In *The National Garden Almanack* (1854) by John Edwards, the firm of Alexander Shanks & Son, from Arbroath in Scotland, advertised an improved machine for mowing grass, which mowed, rolled and collected the cuttings at the same time. It is claimed that the expense of it could be saved in one year.

Also in this book Lord Kinnaird writes with great exactitude of the cost of labour he is saving: 'I have had some months' trial of it, and find that a man and horse, and one woman, can cut and clean upwards of two acres and a half in seven hours, while it formerly took four men and three women nearly three days to put the same ground in order.' The chief gardener to the Duke of Athol shows that he can make an even greater saving, putting more people out of work: 'On our level ground and grass walks we can cut with the Machine in one day nearly as much as eighteen men can cut with scythes.'

The job of gardening was so poorly paid and precarious at the beginning of the nineteenth century that gardeners often had to advertise for charity in the gardening press. In 1839 the Benevolent Institution for the Relief of Aged and Indigent Gardeners and Their Widows was formed to deal with such cases.

In his *Gardener's Magazine* (1826–44) John Loudon, the foremost gardening writer of the first half of the nineteenth century, constantly calls for better wages, hours and lodgings for the hired gardener. He compares an illiterate bricklayer, with wages of between five and seven shillings a day, to a journeyman gardener who, despite having studied geometry, land surveying and botany, received only two shillings and sixpence a day. In 1841 even head gardeners were paid only about a tenth of a cook's salary and half that of a footman. At the end of the nineteenth century a ten-hour day was normal for gardeners. A sixty-hour week was common, with unpaid Sunday duty, and holidays consisting of three feast days a year. Sometimes a day was granted to visit a flower show, but the time usually had to be made up.

Living conditions for gardeners were often atrocious. In his

Encyclopaedia of Gardening (1822) Loudon describes how they lived: 'In one ill-ventilated apartment, with an earthen or brick floor, the whole routine of cooking, cleaning, eating, and sleeping is performed, and young men are rendered familiar with the filth and vermin, and lay the foundation of future diseases, by breathing unwholesome air. How masters can expect any good service from men treated worse than horses, it is difficult to imagine.'

By the end of the twentieth century there were about 200,000 men and 70,000 women agricultural and horticultural workers in Britain. The Ministry of Agriculture, Fisheries and Food distinguished them in the following descending order of pay: foremen, dairy cowmen, all other stockmen, tractor drivers, general farm workers, horticultural workers, females, youths.

Yet every famous garden we have heard about has been dug and planted, weeded and pruned, by workers such as these, usually without any protection from a trade union. Theophrastus had slaves to dig his garden in Athens; the Aztec King Nezahualcoyotl (1403–74) had men from the provinces tending his Texcotzingo gardens as a form of tribute; and medieval monks employed casual labourers to cultivate their monastery gardens. The Botanic Garden in Rio de Janeiro was worked by slave labour up until about 1860 and the Calcutta Botanic Garden used to be cultivated by convicts in chains.

Usually these gardeners have been hidden from history. Even language conspires to conceal them. We hear, for example, of Gertrude Jekyll 'making' her fifteen-acre garden at Munstead Wood, but not of the eleven gardeners she employed; of Ellen Willmott 'making' her garden at Warley Place, near Brentwood in Essex, with no mention of her eighty-six gardeners.

ENCLOSURE AND RESISTANCE

> The man of wealth and pride
> Takes up a space that many poor supplied;
> Space for his lake, his park's extended bounds,
> Space for his horses, equipage and hounds.
> William Goldsmith, 'The Deserted Village' (1769)

The word garden comes from the Old English *geard*, meaning a fence or enclosure, and from *garth*, meaning a yard or a piece of enclosed ground. Enclosure is essential to gardening, and this raises fundamental questions, such as who is doing the enclosing, who owns the land, and who is being kept out.

John Clare, the Northamptonshire poet, recognized this issue. He was a cowherd as a boy and then an under-gardener, and he witnessed the enclosures that took place in England in the early nineteenth century:

> Enclosure came and trampled on the grave
> Of Labour's rights and left the poor a slave.

The history of royal enclosure since 1066 reveals the extent of the theft of common land. By the time of the Domesday Book in 1086 about twenty-five Royal Forests had been established. During the reign of Henry II (1154–89) more than a quarter of the country was subject to the Forest Law, which protected deer, and at the beginning of the eighteenth century many new deer parks were constructed by the gentry. The word lawn was used throughout the eighteenth century to mean a deer park. Instead of an extent of open space and woodland, which could easily be poached, the parks were surrounded by high brick walls and protected by gamekeepers.

Edward Hyams, in *English Cottage Gardens*, has estimated that 'between 1760 and 1867 England's small class of rich men, using as their instrument Acts of Parliament which they controlled through a tiny and partly bought and paid for electorate, stole

seven million acres of common land, the property and the liveli-
hood of the common people of England.'[2]

Marion Shoard arrives at the same figure in her book *This Land
is Our Land*, and she explains what it means: 'Seven million acres
is more than the total area of the following ten contemporary
English counties: Derbyshire, Nottinghamshire, Northamptonshire, Buckinghamshire, Bedfordshire, Hertfordshire, Cambridge, Essex, Norfolk and Suffolk.'[3]

Enclosure of land between 1750 and 1850 involved planting
about 200,000 miles of hedges – at least equal to all those
planted in the previous 500 years. This required a billion plants,
mainly hawthorn, and a prodigious amount of labour to plant
them. Hedges were big business and made fortunes for several
nursery firms.

Such enclosure has always been resisted. Robin Hood and his
outlaws opposed the privatization of the forests. The political
slogan of the Peasants' Revolt of 1381 questioned the exclusive
ownership of land:

> When Adam delved and Eve span
> Who was then the gentleman?

In 1549 the Norfolk uprising against the system of enclosures
was led by Robert Kett who, with an army of 20,000, captured
Norwich, the second city of the country. At the end of the eighteenth century, gangs of armed poachers waged a guerrilla war
all over England against rival gangs of gentry and their gamekeepers. In the nineteenth century public campaigns were necessary to stop Hampstead Heath and Wimbledon Common from
being enclosed for development.

Today, private ownership of land is still a hindrance to people
enjoying the countryside. Almost a third of England's 140,000-
mile footpath network is either difficult or impossible to use
because of obstructions, even though it was given legal protection after the Second World War. A statutory right of way across

the River Nidd in north Yorkshire, for example, has been out of use since the bridge was demolished in 1969. The new bridge, which is gathering dust in a yard in Selby, cannot be erected because one of the landowners will not allow access to his land for its construction.

UTOPIA

> Paradise, and groves
> Elysian, Fortunate Fields – like those of old
> Sought in the Atlantic Main – why should they be
> A history of departed things,
> Or a mere fiction of what never was?
> William Wordsworth, 'The Recluse' (1806)

The division between those who own gardens and those who work in them is evident to those who look. So too is the split between those who do the mental work of planning and design and those who carry out the manual labour of digging and planting, pruning and weeding. However, abolition of this division of labour has sometimes been attempted in revolutionary periods.

William Dell, an army chaplain in Cromwell's New Model Army, wanted to see universities or colleges set up in every city in the country, through which students could work their way whilst still living at home. He had a vision of schools and universities where both intellectual and manual labour would be combined. This idea was behind Marx's proposals for polytechnic education and was also incorporated into the educational programme of the Paris Commune. Similarly in Cuba today, the schools in the country combine the theory and practice of gardening.

The position of the gardener has usually been lowly and despised. As the creator of things of beauty and use, however, the gardener should be honoured, as Wordsworth expresses in 'To

the Spade of a Friend' (1807), 'composed while we were labour-
ing together in his pleasure-ground':

> Thou art a tool of honour in my hands;
> I press thee, through the yielding soil, with pride.

Even in prison, the gardener has the secret of life, as Nelson
Mandela demonstrated: 'A garden was one of the few things in
prison that one could control. To plant a seed, watch it grow, to
tend it and then harvest it offered a simple but enduring satisfaction. The sense of being custodian of this small patch of earth
offered a small taste of freedom.'[4]

At the beginning of the twentieth century in England there
was a movement to introduce gardening into schools. Some of
the proponents were followers of educationalists such as
Rousseau, Pestalozzi and Froebel, with their emphasis on practical learning. But, on the other hand, it was also seen as a way of
preparing working-class boys for agricultural work and stopping
the drift of people from the country to the towns.

As well as bridging the division of labour, gardening can also
unite the academic and the popular. Most gardeners are self-
taught or have learnt from other gardeners, not from an educational institution. At the same time gardening is an opening into
many relevant academic worlds which can be seen to have practical and theoretical purpose – for example botany, anthropology,
linguistics, sociology, history, chemistry, literature, politics,
ecology, art and architecture, to name but a few.

But what remains to be explained is how the monotonous
manual work of gardening can, under certain circumstances, be
pleasurable. This seems strange, for when it is alienated wage
labour, which people are obliged to do, it is usually deadening.
Amateur gardening, however, can destroy the alienation associated with the division of labour. Those who voluntarily sweat
over their own gardens know that even weeding can be fulfilling.
If planning, execution and appreciation of the result are all done
by the same person, the alienation can disappear.

There have always been gardeners who have gardened for themselves and their families, without constraint or orders, uniting design and planning, labour and consumption, although not always ownership. The history of cottage gardens and allotments shows how labourers can spend a whole day doing harsh physical work and still have the energy and enthusiasm to garden in their own time.

Similarly at the end of the eighteenth century, florists' clubs were organized throughout Britain by factory workers and artisans to cultivate flowers. Derbyshire miners raised pansies; Lancashire cotton workers auriculas; Sheffield workers polyanthus; colliers of Northumberland and Durham pinks; Norwich was noted for its carnations; Manchester for gooseberries; Spitalfields in London was famous especially for its tulips; Paisley and Glasgow for pinks.

Gardening can provide a link between the separate spheres of work and leisure. These are so distinct in our culture that it seems strange that people should enjoy work and want to prolong it. A survey in 1948 showed that Aborigines in Arnhem Land collected food every day, whereas if they wished they could have collected enough yams or fish to last for several days. This was because they enjoyed the food expeditions, as they were social outings in which much time was spent talking and resting. The same is true of those who spend the evening working on allotments after a hard day's manual labour.

The Garden of Eden and Paradise are religious utopias, common to Judaism, Christianity and Islam. Etymologically, the word 'utopia' comes from the Greek, meaning nowhere or a place that does not exist. The place may not exist, but the yearning is real. Marx described religion as 'the opium of the people', but he also called it 'the heart of a heartless world'. Gardening often serves a similar purpose as consolation and escape from the world. At the same time, like the church, gardens and gardening are often the expression of power and oppression in the world.

CONTEMPORARY SCENE

> The light of nature will teach us that a common and publicke
> good is to be preferred to all private profit.
>   Samuel Hartlib, *A Designe for Plentie* (1652)

Capitalism and the industrial revolution led to an increasing division of labour. Recently Thatcherism and Blairism have stressed the importance of the market and competition as the driving force in society. Thatcher's belief that there was 'no such thing as society' and her policy of privatization produced increasing private wealth and public squalor. Public parks, for example, continued to decline. The disastrous policy of compulsory tendering and contracting out services to the cheapest bidder led to the devaluing of the skills of horticultural workers, who were often sacked, to be replaced by fewer unskilled workers. There is no statutory obligation on local authorities to maintain public parks, so when the cuts came, the parks were often the first to suffer.

Philips Park in Manchester is a case in point. It was one of the first public parks to be created in England, through subscriptions from working-class and middle-class citizens of the city, opening in 1846. In its heyday, a hundred years ago, it was full of ornate summer bedding. In 1989, when I first visited it, there were only a few bedraggled beds left with a burnt-out car beside them. Several years later I went again, to find the whole park had been grassed over for ease of maintenance. The gardeners had been sacked and the grass was mowed once a week by a contractor. The trees and bushes were all overgrown and women found it unsafe to visit. In recent years there has been an improvement in some parks, but largely because of National Lottery money.

During the same period as the decline in public parks, there was renewed interest in allotments. In 1988 the allotment movement began to grow again for the first time since the Second World War and it was noticeable that allotment holders became more multicultural and there were more women.

City farms began to spread. They began in 1972 with the opening of Kentish Town City Farm, financed by Camden Council, which is still going strong. It introduces city children to farm animals and activities such as horse riding and milking, but also to the animals' interaction with vegetation and types of food. There are plots for growing flowers, fruit and vegetables. There are now about twenty such farms in London and many more around the country.

A growing interest in nature conservancy and ecology has led to the idea of the natural park, like Camley Street, behind Kings Cross station in London, which is internationally renowned, much visited by schools and for the time being saved from demolition by developers. With the nearby canal, it is a haven for wild life and plants, encouraging among young people an interest in natural history.

Similarly the Culpeper Community Garden was developed in the heart of London, near Chapel Market in Islington, the London borough with the smallest area devoted to parks and open spaces. It was designed from a triangle of derelict ground in 1982, with forty-six plots, most held by individuals and families who have no garden. Schools and playgroups also featured among its organic gardeners and three plots were reserved for the disabled. In addition to the plots, a pond with a cascade was built, as well as a lawn and a nature area. The garden provides the opportunity for relaxation: for some it is a regular place to have lunch, for others a sunbathing spot. There are also barbecues and parties for senior citizens, children and local residents.

The community garden movement has also been very strong in the United States, as Sam Bass Warner, Jr. recalls in *To Dwell is to Garden*, which is a history of Boston's community gardens: 'Suddenly, in the spring and summer of 1976, all across the nation, community groups organized and started new community vegetable and flower gardens.'[5]

Even more radical were the temporary gardens made by homeless or impoverished New York City inhabitants, built on 'abandoned, littered lots, bounded by debris', showing 'what homeless people make, not for material comfort, but from social and spiritual need'. In *Transitory Gardens, Uprooted Lives* Diana Balmori goes on to compare these gardens with those of the wealthy that fill the history books: 'Gardens other than those of the wealthy have rarely left a trace. But there are some exceptions – those few gardens that have floated up through history in the line of a poem, the words of a song, or the fragments of a memoir: a small garden outside a medieval city wall; a monastery garden for healing those without any means; a garden leading to a Japanese teahouse, not more than a narrow corridor with a single tree and a few stones, whose very intent was to shun the use of anything costly. It is to these modest examples that we hope to add by capturing the image and material of gardens unique to our own time.'[6] Most of the gardens documented had been destroyed before the book was completed, but they are recorded through Margaret Morton's photographs.

CONCLUSION

> Not in Utopia, subterranean fields,
> Or some secreted island, Heaven knows where!
> But in the very world, which is the world
> Of all of us, – the place where in the end
> We find our happiness, or not at all!
>   William Wordsworth, 'French Revolution' (1804)

At the beginning of the twenty-first century, amateur gardening in Britain is a six to seven billion-pound-a-year industry and gardening programmes on television are very popular. There are ten million keen gardeners. This is the private sphere of conspicuous consumption. At the same time public parks and open spaces are often neglected and gardeners continue to be amongst the lowest-paid workers in the country.

Throughout the world there are still gardeners working in atrocious conditions to provide the West with vegetables and flowers. The 40,000 women working in the Colombian flower industry, for example, are suffering from rheumatism, eczema, damaged embryos, miscarriages, leukaemia, bronchitis, asthma, epilepsy and cancer because of the pesticides that are used. Carnations, roses and chrysanthemums are exported from Colombia to Europe, particularly Aalsmeer, just south of Amsterdam, which is the site of the most important flower market in the world. Millions of flowers are sold there each day, but as one Colombian woman put it: 'Behind every beautiful flower is a death. Flowers grow beautiful while women wither away.'

The competition of the free market may be in the ascendancy, but there has always been an alternative political theory and practice that has emphasized co-operation.

The idea of the garden as an integrated part of a free and equal society is utopian: it does not exist. Nevertheless a continuing horticultural tradition has presented a vision of such gardens and has tried, however partially, to realize it: women healers and radical apothecaries like Nicholas Culpeper; Gerrard Winstanley and the Diggers during the English Revolution of the seventeenth century; cottage gardeners and the working-class florists' societies; Thomas Spence and the movement for public ownership of the land; the allotment movement and land co-operatives; the movement for free public parks in the nineteenth century; William Morris and garden cities; the green and ecology movements; city farms and community gardens. The hallmarks of this tradition are the attempt to integrate beauty and use, town and country, work and leisure, public and private, academic and popular, mental and manual labour.

NOTES

1. James Turner, *The Politics of Landscape*, Oxford, 1979, p. 165.

2. Edward Hyams, *English Cottage Gardens*, London, 1987, p. 158.

3. Marion Shoard, *This Land is Our Land*, London, 1987, p. 66.

4. Nelson Mandela, *Long Walk to Freedom*, London and Boston, 1994, p. 476.

5. Sam Bass Warner, Jr, *To Dwell is to Garden*, Boston, 1987, p. 23.

6. Diana Balmori and Margaret Morton, *Transitory Gardens, Uprooted Lives*, New Haven and London, 1993, p. 2.

GARDENS OF ETHNICITY

Clare Rishbeth

Britain is a multicultural country, but are its gardens? Clare Rishbeth examines how ethnicity informs gardens and gardening, and whether there are any signs of increasing cultural diversity in domestic landscapes.

This essay peers into the back gardens of a multicultural nation. Nine per cent of British residents describe themselves as being from a non-white or mixed-race background, according to the 2001 census. The census fails to report the percentage of this nine per cent who owns a trowel, watch *Gardeners'World* or simply sit out in their gardens on a sunny Sunday afternoon. An unacademic, quantitatively indefensible gut instinct hints that it is less than average. But why have I chosen these particular indicators of garden interest, and what is normal about this average? In looking at the complex relationship between ethnic-community groups, garden design and gardening, am I able to throw light on multiple cultural interpretations of gardens? As the ethnic profile of Britain becomes increasingly diverse, so, perhaps, should our concept of a love of gardens.

As a white woman writing about relationships between ethnicity and gardens, my whiteness is under scrutiny just as much as another's blackness. Ethnicity is more complex than colour, genetic make-up, shared customs or cultures. Most of us experience these in a combination of minority and majority positions, constantly renegotiated as both society and our relationship to it are in flux.

What images are uncovered when I attempt to examine my personal relationship with gardens specifically from the viewpoint of my white British identity? Lawns, tree-climbing, the smell of bonfires, conkers, planting bulbs, bird-tables, outdoor eating, parsley, guinea pigs, washing-lines, privet hedges, ball games and weekend afternoons reading the paper. I realize that the vast majority of these are visual memories directly culled from my childhood photographs. Can I claim them as garden images of my ethnicity, or are they equally gardens of class, of gender, of geography or of educational background? Overarching all of these is an insight into my values, especially those values shared by my family. They point to a value of relaxation, of enjoyment of nature, of socializing, of the garden being an extension of the house. They relate to a private domain in which we are able to exercise choices in pets, in plants and in which we can undertake fairly personal activities.

During the last decade approximately fifteen per cent of new homes built in Britain were apartments. The equivalent figure in France and Germany was fifty per cent. More than any other country in Europe, we seem unable to settle for apartment living, for life without a lawn. A garden is high on the list of househunters' requirements in Britain, the size and aspect of which is weighed up against the quality of the bathroom and the number of bedrooms. To choose to raise a child without a patch of land almost implies wilful neglect of that child's developmental needs.

As a nation, we are mistrustful of the street, wary of uncontrolled associations. Our continental neighbours enthusiastically opt for shared garden spaces in residential developments, making the most of the advantages of scale to have the benefit of doorstep playgrounds, fruit trees, recycling facilities, diverse planting areas and streets that have space for socializing. In Britain we prefer to have small squares of lawn and shrub bed, repeated endlessly along the street, as long as each is within the red line on the property deeds. Ownership and personal control are essential components of our relationship towards our gardens; we are simply not prepared to settle for a life in which the outdoors is entirely shared. We enjoy urban parks and the open countryside (the latter to the point of idolization) but not at the expense of owning our own patch. Despite this emphasis, the density of urban residential housing means that the privacy of the garden is a flawed one. We overlook and overhear our neighbours; we have to tolerate their radios, cats and taste in garden ornaments.

Asian and black communities in Britain appear not to prioritize the garden territory in such a way. The evidence for this is disparate and anecdotal, yet points in a similar direction: generally, people from ethnic-minority backgrounds are less likely to spend time in their gardens and to undertake gardening activities. Non-white faces are conspicuous by their absence on the plethora of gardening programmes; there is no gardening equivalent of Madhur Jaffrey or Benjamin Zephaniah. Sports, cookery, literature and music demonstrate a growing acknowledgement of multicultural influences and encourage, at least in part, involvement of ethnically diverse participants. But visit your local garden centre, and witness a sea of white faces. In *White Teeth*,[1] the defining novel of multi-ethnic north London in the 1990s, gardens and gardening are only introduced as an emblem of the white liberal middle-class family. Despite the action being set in the 'leafy suburbs', the Bengali and Afro-Caribbean participants play out their scenes in cafés, kitchens, streets and parks – never their back gardens. In wandering through city neighbourhoods where there are higher densities of ethnic-community residents, this observation rings true. Compared to similar areas populated primarily by white people, there often appear to be more street-corner conversations, more watching from front doors, more games of street football or cricket. It suggests a cultural comfort in both absolute privacy and absolute community, without the British cultural desire for a semi-private zone that is a compromise between the two.

Wealth is a factor in the leisure activity of gardening. Though there is a gradual shift towards apartment living for aspirant urbanites, in Britain there is still a fairly crude distinction between 'better off' people who live in houses and 'worse off' people who live in flats, the infamous estates of the 1960s onwards. People from ethnic-minority backgrounds are more likely to be unemployed, have lower incomes and live in conditions of poverty than people from white backgrounds. They are also disproportionately housed in urban centres, where there is higher-density housing and high-rise estates. Those who have recently migrated into the United Kingdom from developing countries are generally not in a position to buy accommodation but live in a series of transitions within the rented sector. Migrants are often under significant pressure to earn money to support their immediate family, move to better living conditions, and send money back to the extended family in the home country. Many will also have the desire to move back to their native land at some point in the future.

For people living with these kinds of demands and responsibilities, it is not surprising that even if you have a garden, improving it is low on the list of priorities. Disregarding ethnicity, if you are living on a minimum income or in the rented sector, investing money and time in creating and maintaining an attractive garden is a seemingly illogical activity. In addition, it is often impossible to make substantial purchases without access to a car.

But are there other factors that affect our attachment to gardens, beyond economic circumstance? Earlier I tentatively identified some of my own values and norms, largely formed through my childhood experience, which was spent in a similar climate and culture to that which I live in now. But what of people who have grown up in a country very different to that which they now live in? How are their expectations and values of gardens met and expressed? Is it possible to represent Pakistani, Jamaican or Chinese culture in private gardens?

If cultural symbolism were a significant aspect of gardens belonging to people from migrant background, this essay would be a voyeuristic exploration of exotic sightseeing in a neighbourhood near you. Like a Disney World run out of control, I could have described numerous mini Alhambras in Bradford backyards, tropical jungles in south London and pagodas in Manchester. Garden centres would sell Islamic-style tiling for rectangular water features, and it would be possible to pick up cut-price tubs of bamboo plants in Chinatown. Yet we know this is not real life, and this kind of crude theming generally only happens on garden makeover programmes. This raises two interesting points, with different focuses of ethnicity.

The first is that this actually does happen on garden makeover programmes. For these the target audience is probably described as middle England, predominantly white with disposable income. It isn't at all about people with histories in Asia or the Caribbean negotiating some expression of the ambiguities of dual citizenship. It is everything about the essential ingredient of exotic tourism in white British culture – the outdoor equivalent of eating mangoes, listening to the Buena Vista Social Club and making cushions out of sari fabric.

The aesthetic appeal of the exotic is nothing new, though due to the increase of foreign holidays and the international scope of the media it now impacts a wider range of society. Historical precedents include the Crusaders, who returned from their time in the near East with plants such as the tulip. Botanical collectors have always been obsessed with exotic varieties, seeking out the rare and the flamboyant to please their patrons. The popularity of the Grand Tour inspired the gentry to signify their wealth by their collections and influences from abroad, though tastes were not confined to the direct experience of garden owners. In the

eighteenth to early nineteenth centuries, Chinoiserie was fashionable for both interior and exterior design. The precise nature
of the artwork was sketchy, betraying little understanding of the
differences in culture and religion within the East Asian region.
Egyptian themes were also popular in the nineteenth century,
with garden designs including replica statuary of ancient arte-
facts. An example of both of these pastiche styles can be seen at
Biddulph Grange in Staffordshire. Though we tend to dismiss this
in hindsight as both cultural imperialism and exploitation, the
trend is persistent. Our consumer-led society still uses garden
and home decoration as markers of taste and education, and
these increasingly draw on a response to an appreciation of
diverse cultures, often reworked to appeal to a western aesthetic. Specific styles fade in and out of fashion; currently you are
more likely to be invited round to admire your (white) neighbour's Zen contemplation gravel garden or their Mediterranean
xeriscape than a re-creation of a pagoda.

The second observation is that migrant people often do recreate environments that reflect their cultural heritage, but these
are almost entirely confined to the interiors of their homes.
Several studies in the United States have looked at the interior
styling in homes both of migrants and visiting international students, and described similar phenomena.[2] Objects are displayed
or used which remind the owner of their home country, and also
provide connections with the new life. Items are often invested
with a symbolic importance due to the displacement from previous normality. The built environment can also reflect ethnicity;
in areas where there is a continued strong presence of a migrant
community, the facades and details of the streetscape often bear
witness to the values and aspirations of culture. Chinatowns are
the best-known example of this.

Does this type of symbolism ever find expression in gardens? I
have found no evidence of it in private gardens, though no doubt
there are isolated exceptions. These visual themes usually

develop from gardens of wealth and status, not the vernacular experience of the country of origin, so there is no obvious link to a previous familiar home environment. Other factors could also be connected to climate, expense and the semi-private nature of the garden as opposed to the privacy of the house.

However, there does appear to be an ethnic symbolism present in community gardens in ethnically diverse areas, at times even extending into the public realm of parks. The Casita gardens of New York are an excellent example. These are neighbourhood plots that are managed by local Puerto Rican communities, and reflect in many ways the values and the way of life of the home island. Though primarily reflected in the activities and planting of these gardens, the Puerto Rican identity is also represented by shrines to the Virgin Mary, artwork, flags and 'casita de manderas' (small wooden shacks which are the focus of the Casita's social life). One garden user commented: 'The Casita reminds me of my island. I feel as if I was in Puerto Rico.'[3]

In Britain, some community gardens reflect multicultural themes in response to an ethnically mixed neighbourhood. Chumleigh Gardens, in Southwark, has a series of walled gardens with themes of Oriental, African, Islamic, Mediterranean and English design. It is an attractive and stimulating place, with the educational value of acknowledging the diversity of plants that are grown in Britain. Calthorpe Project community garden in Camden does not have design themes, but uses artwork and allotment plots to engage users from different ethnic backgrounds. Recently opened in Glasgow are the Hidden Gardens, which represent the ethnically mixed local community through the planting, side by side, of native and exotic species of pinus, sorbus and crataegus. Themes from different faith traditions have been subtly incorporated into the design, and celebrations are planned to take place at Eid, Diwali, Christmas and midsummer. None of these gardens was directly designed by people from non-white ethnic communities, though many included a consultation process and inclusive management group. All report a good range of users from different ethnic backgrounds, as well as performing a symbolic role of promoting a multicultural public environment.

Gardens have strong visual qualities, but much of our relationship with our home gardens is activity based: mowing, sunbathing, barbecuing, weeding and hanging out the washing. There is a wide range of individual patterns of behaviour in gardens, and it is reasonable to suggest that some of these differences may be characterized by ethnic background. In the absence of formal research on this topic, it is only possible to draw implications from studies of wider landscapes.

There have been a number of studies, particularly in the United States, which have recorded activities undertaken in parks by members of different ethnic groups. Interviews revealed links between what people valued in park landscapes and their preferred activities. Loukaitou-Sideris's study of parks in Los Angeles observed specific patterns in use by Hispanic communities, who often visited in large groups of families and friends, and congregated round an outdoor meal and children's games.[4] Black users also prioritized the social aspect of park visiting, but were more likely to combine this with sporting activities. The white users tended to visit in smaller groups, individually and in couples, go for walks and to value the naturalistic qualities of the parks. Of particular note were users from the Chinese community, who visited the park in disproportionately low numbers. Those interviewed explained the absence of the Chinese community from the park by describing the Chinese expectation of a park to be like 'a beautiful garden'. The municipal sweep of mown grass and tree cover simply did not attract Chinese people. Another study, focused on an urban Chinese-American community, noted differences between generations of migrants, with first-generation migrants more likely to undertake activities closely associated with patterns of life in China, such as Tai Chi, than later generations born in the United States.[5] Purist theories of assimilation are widely discredited and assume that the majority culture has a fixed identity.[6] However, people who have memories of a very different place and time in their past often find ways of reinterpreting and re-enacting these childhood patterns. Those with shared ethnic roots but who are second-generation citizens rather than migrants will not necessarily place an equal importance on these activities.

In her study of nostalgia and migration, Sylvia Boym identifies an important type of nostalgia in migrant communities that does not simply aim to re-create the past but reinterprets it, acknowledging multiple interpretations, which combine with aspects of the present.[7] The experience of gardens implies this reflective form of nostalgia, requiring engagement with differences in climate, soil and day-to-day activities. Westmacott's study of African-American gardens in the rural south of the United States offers an intriguing insight into values and physical engagement, with the act of gardening set along a complex timeline of migration and land rights.[8] Gardeners interviewed for the study had been born and brought up in the States, but were asked to compare the use and layout of their garden with that of their parents. The garden owners identified a gradual shift in traditions, underpinned by a strong ethos of improvisation and adaptation. The garden previously functioned as an extension of the kitchen, with food preparation and laundry activities being carried out in the yards. The older generations also used to grow medicinal herbs, a practice that has all but died out now. Previously there were no grass areas, so sweeping the yard was a very common chore for African-American children. Lawns are still uncommon in these gardens, though gradually becoming more prevalent.

The African-American culture was not expressed in any symbolic visual form in these gardens, but the decisions and priorities required in long-term garden ownership illustrated underlying values of self-sufficiency, satisfaction of hard work, sanctuary and welcome, and of concern for nature. Gardens often demonstrated a strong sense of ingenuity and adaptation, with the recycling of objects as plant containers, path edging and ornaments. The layout usually included an area of seating by the front door where passers-by could be seen from the road and invited in. Gardeners expressed the joy of 'watching' a garden, and favoured highly coloured reliable annuals over the evergreen foliage shrubs that are dominant in white American garden design. This study illustrates how cultural values can influence the design and management and use of vernacular gardens.

But no area of Britain is like the southern states of the United States. Asians and Afro-Caribbeans setting up home and garden in the United Kingdom face the additional hurdles of inheriting a typical British garden in the typically British climate. Activities that might have been undertaken outdoors in the home country – food preparation, socializing, family picnics, playing – no longer make sense in this erratic, chilly and damp weather. Specific footwear and clothing is required to venture out in at least three seasons of the year. Gardens usually include a lawn, a feature that is both culturally unfamiliar and time-consuming to maintain. Most non-Western cultures value an aesthetic of bright colours, so the predominance of shrubs can be viewed as exceptionally dull. Even the flowers in northern European countries are generally more subtle in colouring and certainly less scented than those that grow in warmer climes. The lack of overpowering, heady scents is particularly disappointing to people who have had the experience of gardenia and frangipani growing outside their doors. There is a lack of accumulated knowledge regarding which plants to buy and when to plant them.

In addition, there is the privacy issue. In interviews I have carried out with Asian women from a range of religious and cultural backgrounds, there appear to be two distinctive patterns of use of outdoor space. Some women described their primary outdoor experience as being in courtyards, which functioned as a combined living and kitchen area – essentially a private domestic environment. Others recounted playing in large communal gardens shared by blocks of apartments, within call of home but without any aspect of privacy. Again, this points to the peculiar nature of the British urban garden as providing neither complete privacy nor freedom of association. Comparable experiences in the United Kingdom are either indoors, or in shared-garden situations.

In recent years there have been a growing number of reports in the media of black and Asian communities involved in allotment plots and productive communal gardens. Many urban regeneration bodies in the United Kingdom promote these initiatives. These are focused on community groups, often single-gender, who meet regularly to cultivate vegetables and herbs usually native to their home country.

The tactile, sensual, immediate experience of familiar plants and soil can unlock memories and prompt intuitive connections with the present. Scents of herbs and flowers are powerfully evocative. Many migrants originate from rural areas, and would have grown up with the feel of soil trickling through the fingers. There is an important sense of continuation of knowledge, of being able to develop skills and adapt techniques to new conditions, thus building confidence. This knowledge can be shared and refined in a context of discussion with people from different cultural backgrounds, as well as those with more expertise of cultivation techniques for a northern European climate. Growing 'exotic' vegetables that are expensive to buy imported can save money and promote healthy eating habits, as well as giving a sense of pride of self-sufficiency.

Communal gardening activity has an important social dimension. Regular meeting and shared experiences with other people who have a similar interest has proved to be highly valued by many migrants, especially those with limited English language skills who can become isolated in an alien and confusing culture.

The act of planting is one of hope, of looking positively to the future. By preparing soil and sowing seeds you devote something of yourself to a place, you make a commitment to it. However you phrase this experience – spiritual, emotional, psychological – it has an ability to shift perspectives. Gardeners move from the comparative state of powerlessness that many migrant groups experience into one where a contribution is being made, an environment is being shaped, an investment is enacted. Which reflects something of the lure of gardening.

The examples discussed here are disparate and offer an inconclusive, half-glimpsed picture of migrant communities and gardens. Yet there is one theme that frequently reoccurs and is given importance whether the situation is a private garden, a shared garden or a public park. This is a love of plants. Individual plant species are frequently mentioned as evocative, meaningful and simply enjoyed. For a Malaysian woman visiting Chumleigh Gardens, it was the rustle of the bamboo that drew her back on repeat visits. 'It reminds me of home.' A Kenyan Indian I interviewed loved growing houseplants, and recounted with pride how she had cultivated tropical-fruit plants from seed. A wide range of community projects across Britain have found that any activity involving planting, such as growing hanging baskets or window boxes, has proved incredibly popular with ethnic groups as diverse as Columbians and Bangladeshis. The Chinese community in Glasgow who advised on the Hidden Gardens planting scheme specifically recommended flowering cherries, which had particular significance in their culture. The Black Environmental Network pioneered the idea of multicultural gardens in schools, so that children from different cultures can see how plants found growing in normal British back gardens originated from all over the world. Is it symbolism, is it nostalgia, or is it the way that plants directly engage our senses of touch, scent and sight? The answer will be as individual as the people that tend and admire them. But what is increasingly clear is that it is through plants that we find a common connection between people of different ethnic backgrounds. The activity of gardening, the pet guinea pigs, the semi-private world of privet hedges and sunbathing may differentiate us, may prove to be an aspect of British culture that fails to connect with gardens owners from Asian and African backgrounds. But the rose, the coriander, the geranium and the pine – these might unite us.

NOTES

1. Zadie Smith, *White Teeth*, London, 2000.

2. H. Bir, 'The Meanings of Objects in Environmental Transitions: Experiences of Chinese Students in the United States', *Journal of Environmental Psychology* 1992, 12, pp. 135–47 and S. Boym, *The Future of Nostalgia*, New York, 2001.

3. D. Winterbottom, 'The Creation of Cultural/Social Spaces in the Barrios of New York City', Environmental Design Research Association Annual Conference, 4–8 March 1998, p. 91.

4. A. Loukaitou-Sideris, 'Urban Form and Social Context: Cultural Differentiation in the Uses of Urban Parks', *Journal of Planning Education and Research*, 1995, 14, pp. 89–102.

5. T.W. Zhang and P.H. Gobster, 'Leisure preferences and open space needs in an urban Chinese American community', *Journal of Architectural and Planning Research*, 1998, 15/4, pp. 338–55.

6. B. Parekh, *Rethinking Multi-culturalism*, Basingstoke, 2000.

7. S. Boym, *The Future of Nostalgia*, New York, 2001.

8. R. Westmacott, 'The Gardens of African-Amercians in the Rural South' in J.D. Hunt and J. Wolschke-Bulmahn (eds), *The Vernacular Garden*, Dumbarton Oaks, 1993.

THE EXPLOSION OF GARDEN VISITING IN FRANCE

Louisa Jones

France has seen an exponential increase in the number of gardens opening to the public, together with burgeoning public interest in gardening. The author teases out some prevailing themes – some with positive effects on the scene, others with negative.

Garden making and garden visiting have both increased dramatically in France in the past fifteen years. Individual and community initiatives are now attracting ever-stronger official and commercial recognition. Four ministries manage French parks and gardens: those of culture, tourism, agriculture, and ecology and sustainable development (formerly environment). In 2003, a national garden council, composed half of government, half of private association representatives and personalities, was founded to co-ordinate protection, creation and promotion. In the same year, a government tourist association (AFIT) published a detailed survey on garden tourism. Already in 2002, L'IESA, a prestigious private art institute training 'cultural engineers': administrators, auctioneers, publicists, created a new diploma in the 'mise en tourisme du patrimoine vert'– the opening up to tourism of France's garden capital.

The green heritage includes châteaux parks, both the formal layouts associated in English minds with the French style, and the irregular landscaped parks of later periods. Historic botanical gardens, arboreta and plant collections are also numerous. The kitchen garden or *potager* is now a proudly acknowledged genre, subject of study for French ethnologists who use the term *jardin ordinaire* (ordinary garden) to cover everything from peasant plots to the industrial allotments created after 1896. In the past 150 years, urban parks and a range of middle-class domestic styles of garden have also proliferated (both of which provided subjects for Impressionist painters). In our time, people of all backgrounds have been creating idiosyncratic gardens that involve every imaginable site, budget and taste. Large numbers of them have opened to the public.

Garden visiting began in France after World War II when a network of private owners, mainly aristocratic collectors, began organizing visits among themselves. To the Mallets and Princess Sturdza of Varengeville, Prince Wolkonsky, Bernard de la Rochefoucauld, Charles de Noailles, the Gérard family and others we owe the creation in 1973 of the influential Association des Parcs Botaniques de France. This dedicated group instigated an inventory of woody plants, the establishment of national collections and the famous biannual plant fair at the Château de Courson, where at first there was debate as to whether plants should be actually sold or simply offered for exchange. Courson still prides itself on favouring quality over salesmanship. In that same decade Anne-Marie Cousin and Michel Racine initiated an inventory of French gardens sponsored by the new Mission du paysage (the landscape commission at the Ministry of Environment). This has resulted in a file of some ten thousand gardens, half of which were judged to be 'remarkable' for 'historic, botanical or design reasons'. About 1,600 of them have been officially listed. In 1988 the Ministry of Culture started a campaign called 'Visiter un jardin en France', but this lost steam after 1995 when its administration (and the budget) was transferred to the regions. Today the Ministry of Culture is again promoting garden visiting all over the country as an important component of two annual open-house weekends (the 'Rendez-vous au jardin' programme).

Many of the finest new gardens, however, grew up in remote provinces and wild landscapes, and Parisians did not immediately notice them. The most frequently cited guide to French gardens, compiled by the same Michel Racine, ignored some of these completely in its first edition.[1] The best witnesses to change in French home gardening through the years have been journalists. The fiftieth anniversary issue of the railway workers' gardening magazine (*Jardins du cheminot*) nicely summarized evolution between 1943 and 1993: after the desperate war years, ornamental gardening was like white bread, a welcome luxury. Lawns replaced vegetable plots, new American dahlias and delphiniums filled up borders, anything that moved was zapped with a chemical. By the 1990s however, even conservative railway workers were replacing lawns with wildflower meadows, planting artichokes among the roses, sparing a plot of nettles to make home-brew liquid fertilizer. Visits are not mentioned, but the magazine speaks to and for a close-knit gardening community where neighbourly exchanges have always been the rule.

Middle-class French gardeners have for decades read *Mon Jardin ma maison* and *L'Ami des jardins*. Both magazines have produced guides or surveys of home gardens, which give a more accurate picture than the official publications. Their journalists scour the country regularly. Photographer Georges Lévêque was a pioneer in this effort in the 1970s, when the model of gardening recommended to readers was resolutely English. Lévêque and his colleagues did much to educate French gardeners about plants, but the French examples then presented were idealized, anonymous and inaccessible. Today, each garden featured in these glossy pages is specifically situated, linked to its site and region. Often visiting conditions are provided. As for style, the mixed border has lost ground to natural gardening, plant collecting and new forms of 'land art'.

In the mid-1990s I visited the Jardins de l'Albarède, made by Serge and Brigitte Lapouge. Both were unemployed at the time, busy fixing up a property inherited from her family. I noted a dead tree trunk – not removed as unsightly as it would have been in the 1950s, not left to house wildlife as in the 1970s, but discreetly painted in teal-blue stripes. It was leaning over a fountain that Serge had sculpted out of local stone. Today L'Albarède belongs to a successful network of visitable gardens in the Dordogne. Serge has become a self-styled and successful designer and Brigitte writes the ornamental-garden advice column for France's oldest organic gardening magazine, *Les Quatre Saisons*. This couple represents a new approach to gardening which combines ecology, homemade art and a desire to share both with other gardeners and with the public at large.

NATURE, ART AND THE *'TERROIR'*

France's leading ecologist is Gilles Clément, who lectures widely and always to a full house of young enthusiasts. He lives half the year in his own secluded country garden but his many public creations can be visited all over France (for example Paris, Blois, Lille, Valloires, Vulcania). He is consultant for the effective waterfront conservancy agency (Conservatoire du littoral) and created for them the Domaine du Rayol near Hyères on the Mediterranean coast, an experimental 'planetary' garden recreating Mediterranean biotopes from all over the world. He laid out with his own hands parts of the gardens of the Le centre Terre vivant at Le domaine de Raud in the Alps, France's equivalent of the British organic pioneers the Henry Doubleday Foundation.

Clément is also a novelist, philosopher and professor at the prestigious landscape architecture school at Versailles (L'Ecole nationale supérieure du paysage de Versailles). Here he defends biodiversity and enlightened home gardening as a model for land management. He has for years been a lone voice against a landscape architecture establishment famous for its conceptualism, its emphasis on public projects and its dismissal of private gardens as bourgeois escapism. Many of these formalists are

now changing their minds, however – not so much in response
to ecology but because of the contemporary recognition of gardens as a form of art. This new legitimacy makes even the private garden worthy of both professional attention and public
notice. The latter often takes the form of exhibitions and visits.

The Chaumont Landscape and Garden Festival has been
instrumental in helping the general public connect gardens with
art. The atmosphere is experimental, irreverent, educational and
playful all at once. Children are welcomed at Chaumont and
adults are encouraged, through garden art, to rediscover the
children inside themselves. Many 'installations' encourage active
participation, and one reviewer in Britain's *Garden Design Journal*
advised parents to bring a change of clothing for their offspring.
At the same time, Chaumont attracts plasticians who view art as
process, as event, as group endeavour. The convergence has
spread: sculpture gardens, both ephemeral and permanent, featuring works created on site or incorporating the site, are now
opening all over France. Cézanne's studio in Aix now features
temporary installations every summer in its wood. The festival of
Barbirey in Burgundy stresses performing arts in dialogue with
gardens. Even the most traditional gardens now feature seasonal
events to encourage visitors to return often: Easter egg hunts for
children, jam tastings, craft workshops, nature walks, plant fairs
and so on.

French gardens have thus become less private, more linked to
social activity and community identity. Spirit of place here
implies the *terroir*, a rural area characterized by its own landscapes, food, crafts, building styles, even language. Jean Cabanel
of the Mission du paysage counted roughly 600 distinct *terroirs* in
France, ranging from Flemish to Mediterranean. This diversity
has long made France a major tourist destination. Today, in all
regions, villages express their identity in gardenesque traffic
roundabouts – affirmations of local pride also intended as a siren
call to tourists. Rural enthusiasm is not limited to roundabouts,

however. Marie-Paule Baussan, the only 'cultural engineer' in France to specialize in gardens, reports that numerous communities now want to transform waste spaces into public gardens in the hopes that minimal investment will fill the town's coffers. 'It has become a regular cream puff', she says resignedly. 'They rarely plan on upkeep. I sometimes tell them to put in a child-care centre or a swimming pool instead.' Some ventures have, however, made some small towns famous, if not rich. The Jardins pour la Terre at Arlanc in the Cantal is a low-budget project: a park laid out as a map of the world displays plants introduced into the Auvergne from each continent, and the gardeners are recruited from the long-term unemployed. At the other end of the scale, the stunning Jardins de l'Imaginaire (main designer Kathryn Gustafson) were commissioned by the mayor of the Dordogne town of Terrasson. It cost millions but draws visitors from all over the world. Both projects link a global theme to local sites. Celebration of the *terroir* is not necessarily reactionary. Like the roundabouts, it affirms local identity and reaches out to the world at the same time.

WHO OPENS AND HOW?

Outside Paris, the Loire Valley châteaux receive the most visitors: Chenonceau has 841,000 per year and Villandry 363,000 per year, for example. The nearby Chaumont festival indexes its prices on these competitors but peaks at 150,000. Its director, Jean-Jacques Pigeat, points out that the festival is supported by its winter training facilities. Originally created with heavy regional funding, Chaumont is becoming autonomous thanks to its growing design-consultancy business. The bamboo gardens at Prafrance, north of Nîmes, have long been a popular favourite, a family endeavour open since the 1950s despite many setbacks. They welcome some 350,000 visitors a year in spite of a remote location, and survive thanks to their nursery and shop.

About half the gardens noted in the recent survey are family nurseries. Most were started by people in other jobs who were seduced by a passion for plants: the Lemonniers at the Jardins de Bellevue in Normandy, for example, who now have national collections of hellebores and meconopsis; Eléonore Cruse in the Ardèche with her hundreds of heirloom roses in a wild mountain landscape; Monique Hégo at Berchigrange in the Lorraine; the Jardin-Plume in Normandy; or the Jardin Roman of Monique Lafon in Burgundy, to name but a few of the most original gardens created by collectors. Today the small nurseries have their own very active association. It is former nurserymen who founded France's most ebullient garden newspaper, *Le Gazette des jardins*.

Owners of historic monuments have often, here as elsewhere, opened their gardens in the hope of helping cover restoration costs. Many first aimed at period style but have now turned to contemporary design: the Château of Bosmelet in Normandy with its striking rainbow *potager* or Yvoires on Lake Geneva, where designer Alain Richert created the imaginative Labyrinthe des cinq sens (labyrinth of the five senses). These two successful examples have emerged from an array of more banal efforts. Some impoverished châteaux owners first looked to their kitchen gardens as a fast way of creating instant public appeal. Then, faced with intensive upkeep, they turned to 'gardens for the five senses', a mix of medieval inspiration and formal herb arrangements – easier to maintain and almost as fast to produce. Small towns have sometimes chosen this model for the same reasons. There too the successful examples – Cahors, Uzès, La Garde Adhémar – stand out among the many trite imitations.

Gardens created in the hope of making money rarely succeed, aesthetically or financially. The best new public gardens are unclassifiable. Their creators are idealistic young people, such as the two unemployed architects, Patrick Taravella and Sonia Lesot, who created Le Prieuré d'Orsan in the Berry. La Sedelle and Les Jardins de la Forge in the Creuse have similar histories – the first a broad landscape featuring a national collection of maples, the second a series of small wild gardens. These examples have almost become symbols of the new gardening spirit in France.

Only a handful of French gardens actually cover costs. A comparison of two profitable private ventures in the Dordogne reveals some new trends. Both gardens are famous for virtuoso pruning of green forms. Patrick Seramadiras loves recounting how his father designed the gardens at Eyrignac after refusing submissions by Russell Page and Loup de Viane. A photographer – Georges Lévêque, of course – was allowed to visit in 1986 on condition that he did not publish. Visitors were admitted as of 1990 – just 700 that first year. Seramadiras used to invite them to join him in the swimming pool. He showed the garden himself and asked payment only of those guests he did not like. Then he allowed a twelve-page spread in *Le Figaro* magazine and visitors increased in one year from 5,000 to 25,000. Seramadiras owns an advertising agency, which manages billboards on Paris streets. Whenever one is empty, he puts up posters of his garden. The result today is 80,000 visitors yearly, but he still loves to sell tickets himself. He wonders why the local tourist office never helps him out.

Journalists are now warmly welcomed at Eyrignac. But when I was sent to visit by the *Sunday Telegraph* magazine, nearby Marqueyssac was chosen as a subject instead. It is owned, along with two other local châteaux, by another businessman who remains in the background. Its restoration is far more recent and designed for public use. Laid out along a promontory with dramatic views on three sides, its park can be visited along one of three paths, each with its own character and degree of difficulty. Architecture, garden and landscape have been beautifully blended. At Marqueyssac, visitors do not have to tour in guided groups as at Eyrignac. The service facilities are not separate, obvious and ugly but well integrated, easily accessible from within the garden and fun. The gardens at Marqueyssac are inseparable from their site whereas at Eyrignac, although very elegant, they seem set upon empty green space. In the former there is a sense of participation and discovery, whereas at Eyrignac almost everything, even the new rose garden, is immediately visible. One remains outside throughout, a spectator. Eyrignac recently got three stars in the Michelin guide but Marqueyssac is far more typical of current French garden design for public use. I overheard the head gardener there giving instructions on how to improve a path for the use of prams.

WHO VISITS AND WHY?

The AFIT survey claims that only fifteen per cent of visitors to French gardens are foreigners. But although home gardening has become a national pastime, the French do not visit to 'steal' ideas. Nor to get a closer look at the gentry. Nor even to buy plants. And garden visiting in France – by the French – is not, above all, an activity for the retired and elderly. I would venture (without statistics to hand) to say that it is largely a family activity, an opportunity for weekend outings with children in which participation counts as much as spectatorship. In visiting a garden together, families enjoy nature and culture combined. Garden advertising stresses both play and education (*ludique* and *pédagogique* are complementary terms in the new rhetoric).

Two 'discovery' parks in wild mountain areas illustrate variations on this theme. One is the Centre d'art of La Vassivière near Limoges, in a summer resort area. Its outdoor sculpture collections (including works made for the site by artists of the stature of David Nash and Andy Goldsworthy) were established in the 1970s. When I went there in June some years ago, I found local families fishing, boating and lying in the sun while art tourists admired the sculpture park. But at the Vallon du

Villaret, established around 1990 in the even more remote Lozère, the same people were enjoying the outdoors, playing with sculpture designed for visitor participation and following game signals, which taught them about local fauna. In just ten years, the Vallon has reached an annual visitor figure of 50,000, and it appeals to a public aged from seven to seventy, advertising both at campsites and at art museums. It is so well designed that even when the car park is full of coaches you can walk alone, hearing only birdsong and distant children's laughter. It is the creation of a talented young man, Guillaume Sonnet, who describes it as 'anti-Disney'. La Vassivière is now under new direction and one of its main aims is to unite its two publics, under consultation with Gilles Clément.

The Paradise gardens of Cordes-sur-Ciel, created by Arnaud Maurières and Eric Ossart on land rented from the town, attract an equally mixed audience. On these bright and busy terraces, local peasants rediscovering the vegetables of their youth meet international garden journalists. Maurières and Ossart have influenced urban parks all over France. As head gardener and teacher at the Conservatoire international des parcs et jardins et paysage de Chaumont-sur-Loire, Ossart developed a new planting style called 'le nouveau fleurissement' – highly coloured but loose-knit, mixing edibles with annuals, perennials and grasses. Their creations can be seen in Paris (Musée de Cluny), Blois, Orléans, Lyons and Toulouse. The terraces at Cordes allowed them to experiment and to meet their public personally, which they love to do. Most new gardens, whatever their style, cultivate this wide appeal: at La Sedelle, owner Philippe Wanty receives *Vogue* journalists and carloads of *gendarmes* with their families on the same day.

Do *Vogue* journalists and *gendarmes* want the same things from a garden? Experienced owners agree that the French public still expects flowers. The Conseil national des villes et villages fleuris sends scouting teams out to award prizes all over France, and publishes a guide of the results. Young designers sometimes deplore its window-box influence on grass-roots taste while acknowledging that its national organizers appreciate more contemporary trends.

Good taste has its dangers, too: it may become too familiar, too identified with tradition. The historic floral parks and gardens of Normandy – truly wonderful – sometimes seem tame today compared with younger, more experimental efforts. Interest has shifted to other regions. The Centre-Loire region, with its famous châteaux, has a highly active garden association with a truly professional website. Riviera officialdom, after years of infighting, is sponsoring its fabulous heritage more intelligently (though western Provence, with its dozens of new designer gardens, remains the most private region in France). The *département* to watch is the Moselle where a young gardener called Pascal Garbe has set up a network of fourteen sites called Jardins sans limites (gardens without limits) in collaboration with a province in nearby Germany. This kind of European initiative will surely develop elsewhere before long. Serre de la Madone, Lawrence Johnston's Riviera garden, is already twinned with Hidcote.

THE FUTURE

More and more private garden owners want visitors. More and more associations now exist with the joint aim of organizing visits among members and advising those who intend to go public. The French Heritage Association, Les Demeures historiques, and of course the Garden History Society all encourage French owners by awarding prizes. The most complete network is the Comité des parcs et jardins de France, with active branches in each region of France.

The Ministry of Culture also provides workshops to help owners open their gardens, though it prefers to speak of 'mise en valeur' (development) rather than tourism. Jean-Pierre Bady, president of the new Conseil national des jardins, immediately links this *valorisation* to pedagogy. Officially, then, gardens remain cultural and educational. The Ministry is now progressing from preservation and protection of gardens to contemporary creation. It is currently commissioning works by named designers for nine historic sites, a programme perhaps inspired by the Moselle. A new label, 'jardin remarquable', will be conferred on deserving efforts. In practice, all levels of government – regional, departmental, local – are now concentrating hard on garden promotion. In some cases they work wonders; in others, they are unbelievably obstructive. Rarely in any public project is there an adequate budget for maintenance. Visitors have difficulty getting clear information. Designer names are omitted nearly everywhere, even in official publications. Tourist offices are often the last to know, even when their own regional administrators have published garden brochures (also rarely available). Websites list 'nature' (read 'sports') and 'culture' but even on the official Ministry of Culture site, it is very difficult to find any information about its garden projects.

Private efforts are not always any more successful. Attempts to organize regional networks for tourist promotion have often met with prohibitive internal rivalries. The very rich are just beginning to consider gardens as cultural investment, which might lead to tax write-offs. Unfortunately a particularly ambitious project, which might have been a model, has ended disastrously. This was the great water park of Méry-sur-Oise, a combined effort of landscape architects Pascal Cribier and Lionel Guibel with botanist Patrick Blanc. The patron was Vivendi, which went bankrupt. The park, which requires six full-time gardeners, is now deteriorating, its fate still undecided. It was arguably one of the most original and beautiful public gardens of Europe, but only for a very short time.

Some of the official confusion can be blamed on the intense pace of current transitions. We may look back with regret later on when everything has become commercially streamlined. Meanwhile, though garden visiting in France helps preserve a threatened heritage, it is not being experienced as nostalgia. The new movement belongs to young idealists whose estrangement from official politics has turned into a strong associative movement. Legislation encouraging non-profit associations makes it possible for anyone wanting to open a garden, organize a plant fair or set up a course, to get tax breaks. Many rural projects have survived thanks to this associative status, including the Jardins d'Elie, the botanic gardens of a homespun philosopher-shepherd in the Var, saved, for the moment, by a group of young volunteers.

The best efforts are personal and unclassifiable, such as the celebrated vertical wall gardens of Patrick Blanc, many of which can be visited. The young, who insist on combining head and hands, design and dirt, explore various avenues: Benoit Bourdeau, head gardener at Serre de la Madone in Menton, has become an expert in the management of public gardens; Jean Laurent Felizia, founder of the design group Mouvement et paysages, combines creation and maintenance; Bruno Marmiroli and Patrick Genty, designers of the famous Palestine wall exhibit at Chaumont, now specialize in community projects; Rémy Duthoit, a former Clément student, combines landscape architecture with sculpture involving wind patterns; Marc Nucera, trained as a pruner, became a sculptor of trees and landscapes; nurseryman Philippe Brande in the Dordogne opened a wild part of his property to designers of imaginative tree houses. These 'gardenists' have precarious careers, all the more so those who specialize in the growing movement of shared gardens (*jardins partagés*) for the disabled, the homeless or the long-term unemployed. So it is with Natacha Guillaumont in Marseille, who works with the Fondation Abbé Pierre and the Institut des jeunes aveugles (Institute for the Blind). Gardens in France are strongly associated in the public mind with helping people learn, especially children. Yet in spite of confusion, and the dangers of bureaucracy and commercialization, there is a wonderful wind of creativity and enthusiasm here. It is a good time to discover gardens in France.

NOTES

1. Michel Racine, *Jardins en France*, Arles, 1997.

DIGGING FOR ANARCHY

Tom Hodgkinson

The author, a smallholder, traces the radical tradition of vegetable gardening in Britain, from the eighteenth-century Diggers to 1970s punk-anarchists CRASS, to the present day.

Following a recent move from west London to a tumbledown farmhouse in North Devon, I decided to follow in the steps of Hugh Fearnley-Whittingstall and start my own vegetable patch. In the morning my various London-based media projects, undertaken for large companies, would collapse in a mess of lawyers, anguished phone calls and angry e-mails. But in the afternoon, I would trudge up to my little patch of earth and dig, rotavate, work in cow muck and build raised beds. At night I would go to bed with *The Vegetable Expert* by I.R. Hessayon, and confuse myself by reading about a new world of brassicas, humus, seed beds, earthing up, blanching and rotation.

My first step was to plant a few rows of radishes in March. One month later, I pulled the edible vegetables from the ground. For a seed to grow and bear fruit is of course the most natural and ordinary thing in the world. But to me, the process was nothing short of magical. It filled me with wonder, amazement and a deep sense of satisfaction that I had grown something for myself – virtually for free – which I could then feed to my family. They looked like radishes, they tasted like radishes, they were radishes. And just a few weeks previously they had been tiny dots.

The radishes were followed by beetroot, potatoes, some hilariously misshapen carrots, rocket, onions, garlic, peas, beans, courgettes. The sense of pride when I came back into the kitchen bearing an overflowing basket of the most delicious vegetables in the world was tremendous. And at a time in my life when everything in work was going wrong, here was something that worked. In the middle of the post-industrial society, with its frustrations and toil, I felt I had created a little patch of paradise.

I started to reflect that the fun and pleasure of growing your own vegetables is not solely related to the satisfaction of pulling a turnip from the earth, although that is a marvellous feeling. There is more to it than that. There is a special, deep pleasure that comes from a sudden feeling of freedom. Growing your own means that in a small way you have escaped the constrictions of the wage economy, whereby we specialize in one activity to the exclusion of all others and then pay other people to specialize in something else. In maintaining your own patch of earth, you escape the world of money, governments, supermarkets and the industrial processes of food production. Suddenly Jack and the Beanstalk looks like a parable about self-sufficiency. The beans are indeed magic because they lead to independence for Jack and his mother. Start with a few beans and you will soon find bounty hanging from the branches and growing under the ground.

In this sense, then, digging is literally anarchy. It is anarchy in action. Anarchy consists in essentially ignoring the state and the empty promises of democracy. It consists in refusing to give up your authority to an external party. It means refusing to wait until governments 'sort it out', and it means starting to sort things out for yourself.

C.S. Lewis, in his 1958 essay, 'Willing Slaves of the Welfare State', cited the bloody-minded Renaissance essayist Montaigne as an example of a free man. In this piece, Lewis attacks the centralizing tendencies of government, which, as he saw it, were stripping the English 'freeborn mind' of its independence:

> I believe a man is happier, and happy in a richer way, if he has 'the freeborn mind.' But I doubt whether he can have this without economic independence, which the new society is abolishing. For economic independence allows an education not controlled by the Government; and in adult life it is the man who needs, and asks, nothing of the Government who can criticize its acts and snap his fingers at its ideology. Read Montaigne; that's the voice of a man with his legs under his own table, eating the mutton and turnips raised on his own land. Who will talk like that when the State is everyone's schoolmaster and employer?

For centuries, the battle for the land has been at the centre of radical politics in this country. There is a long tradition that links earth and anarchy. In 1649, the cattle herdsman Gerard Winstanley led six helpers to dig the common land at St George's Hill, Weybridge, in a protest against serfdom and private property. They became known as the Diggers. When Winstanley and his partner John Everard were called before the authorities, in the shape of Lord Fairfax, to explain themselves, they refused to take off their hats because, they said, '[Fairfax] was but their fellow creature.' The court report relates that

> there had lately appeared to [Everard] a vision, which bad him arise and dig and plough the earth, and receive the fruits thereof... their intent is to restore the Creation to its former condition. That as God promised to make the barren land fruitful, so now what they did was to restore the ancient community of enjoying the fruits of the Earth, and to distribute the benefits thereof to the poor and needy, and to feed the hungry and to clothe the naked.

Various landlords tried to force the Diggers off the land by brute force. They moved to nearby Cobham where, by April 1650, they had eleven acres of corn and had built seven houses. Again, they were rounded upon by the authorities. Their houses were burnt down. Winstanley went on to write various pamphlets such as 'The True Leveller's Standard Advanced', 'The New Laws of Righteousness' and 'The Law of Freedom in a Platform', which outlined his anarchist philosophy. 'Reason', he wrote, 'requires that every man should live upon the increase of the earth comfortably.'

In 1759, the philosophical quest of Voltaire's *Candide* ends with the hero concluding simply: 'Il faut cultiver notre jardin.' You can travel round the world, you can take loads of drugs, you can read poetry, indulge in weird sex, but at the end of it all, you must look after your own garden.

In the nineteenth century it was the turn of William Cobbett to promote the advantages of independent living. In *Cottage Economy: Containing Information Relating to the Brewing of Beer, Making of Bread, Keeping of Cows*, he gives practical advice to families on how to look after themselves. This is because he had been appalled by what he saw in the 1820s when travelling around Britain, as documented in *Rural Rides*. The old rural culture of self-reliance was being destroyed by a boring, tedious monoculture based around specialization, factories, economies of scale and divisions of labour.

Later in the nineteenth century, the rural radical John Ruskin took up Cobbett's project. 'In the true Utopia,' he wrote, 'man will rather harness himself, with his oxen, to his plough, than leave the devil to drive it.' Putting his money where his mouth was, Ruskin in 1877 founded a community called St George's Farm at Totley near Sheffield, populated by a group of shoemakers who sought self-government. The scheme failed, but attracted the attention of Edward Carpenter, a young radical who became friends with like-minded souls such as W.B. Yeats, the anarchist Peter Kropotkin, and William Morris. All were inspired by Ruskin's 'rustic vision', as well as by Henry David Thoreau's *Walden*, that great American hymn to self-reliance. All were convinced of the evil of the wage system, the need for variety and pleasure in work and of the importance of digging. Here is William Morris in his 1884 lecture, 'Useless Work Versus Useless Toil':

> To compel a man to do day after day the same task, without any hope of escape of change, means nothing short of turning his life into prison-torment. Nothing but the tyranny of profit-grinding makes this necessary. A man might easily learn and practise at least three crafts, varying sedentary occupation with outdoor-occupation calling for the exercise of strong bodily energy for work in which the mind had more to do. There are few men, for instance, who would not wish to spend part of their lives in the most necessary and pleasant of all work, cultivating the earth.

For G.K. Chesterton, who was appalled at the way the ruling classes had removed the men, women and children from the land and put them in soul-destroying factories for fourteen hours a day, the answer lay in what he called Distributism, or Peasant Proprietorship. This was the idea that every household in the country should have at least an acre of land to itself, wherefrom the family could furnish itself with the essentials of living. They would keep pigs, a cow, goats, ducks, poultry; they would be independent, in part, at least, from wages and therefore of mill owners and government.

Another bold pioneer in this field was D.H. Lawrence. In a letter of 18 January1915 to a friend, he wrote of his dream: 'To gather together about twenty souls and sail away from this world of war and squalor and found a little colony where there shall be no money but a sort of communism as far as necessaries go, and some real decency.' There is something touchingly wide-eyed about Lawrence's faith, particularly when his experiments appeared doomed to failure. At the end of 1915 he moved to Cornwall, where, he wrote: 'I knew it was the Promised Land, and that a new heaven and earth would take place.' Soon though, Lawrence moved back to Hampstead. And then he planned to move to the Andes. 'It has become so concrete and real, the Andes plan, it seems to occupy my heart', he wrote in 1918. But in fact he went to Ceylon. And then to Australia, and New Mexico, before returning to England. It has to be said that his plan never worked, inspiring though it was.

More recently, the late John Seymour, who died in 2004 at the age of ninety, had terrific success in 1976 with his book *Self-Sufficiency*, the first book to be put together by that dynamic duo, Dorling and Kindersley. Cobbettesque in its ambitions, the book gives directions on growing vegetables, keeping stock, making baskets and bricks, brewing beer and even weaving and pottery. Seymour urges city-dwellers to tear up their bourgeois lawns and perennials and plant cabbages in their place. He counsels growing sunflowers for their oil and seeds; in other words, he wants your garden to be both beautiful and useful. In his fore-word to the book, E. F. Schumacher places the handbook in the tradition of anarchic self-reliance:

> We can do things for ourselves or we can pay others to do them for us. These are the two 'systems' that support us; we might call them the 'self-reliance system' and the 'organisation system' . . . in the modern world, during the last two hundred years or so, there has been an enormous and historically unique shift: away from self-reliance and towards organisation. As a result people are becoming less self-reliant and more dependent than has ever been seen in history. They may claim to be more highly educated than any generation before them; but the fact remains they cannot really do anything for them-selves. They depend utterly on vastly complex organisations,

on fantastic machinery, on larger and larger money incomes . . .
contrariwise, nothing can stop the flowering of a society that
manages to give free rein to the creativity of its people – *all* its
people. This cannot be ordered and organised from the top. We
cannot look to government, only to ourselves, to bring about
such a state of affairs.

Then even more recently we have the example of the 1980s
anarchist punk band CRASS. As well as encouraging people to
wear black, protest against Mrs Thatcher and spray anarchy signs
on bus-stops, they established their own commune on a rented
property an hour outside central London. On their acre of land,
they established a vegetable patch combined with a sort of
underground arts centres for events, workshops and confer-
ences. Commentators at the time were confused: did they want
to overthrow the state or grow cabbages? What the commentators didn't see, of course, is that these are one and the same
thing. When I went to interview Penny Rimbaud of the group, he
was on the roof, mending tiles, a demonstration of self-reliance
in action.

Today, the example of Hugh Fearnley-Whittingstall shows the
positive results of moving a glib media wally from London into
the country and giving him a spade. He did it as an experiment
for a television show but became hooked, and good luck to him.
The problem with Whittingstall – who I actually revere as a positive force and great inspiration – is that all too easily, thanks to
television, his project can be reduced to a 'lifestyle', to mere
entertainment: fun to watch but stripped of all political content
or even practical relevance.

In contemporary popular culture, the freedom-seeking pop
group the Libertines has reawakened talk of Albion, of the need
to create one's own paradise, to forge Jerusalem on this earth.
And I notice that Delia Smith's book on growing your own vegetables is a bestseller at the time of writing. So it's clear that the

thirst is there. We are fed up with boredom and slavery. So down your weapons, revolutionaries, and pick up your spades. Digging is fun and freedom all rolled into one.

LANDSCAPE DESIGN AND THE BIOSPHERE
Conflict or Complicity?

Gilles Clément
translated and edited by Louisa Jones

Gardeners, landscape designers and others who deal with space must remember that the material they engage with is living. A purely architectural or technical approach is simply not enough, argues the leading French landscape designer and writer.

Landscape design – a relatively recent addition among the professions dealing with space, historically speaking – has one peculiarity that distinguishes it from the rest: it deals with living beings.

Nothing prevents urban planners, architects, geographers or artists in various media from doing this also. There are those whose curiosity leads them in this direction, but they have a choice, whereas the landscape designer, on the contrary, is expected always to work directly with nature. A landscape project requires a list of the species to be included as part of a vision in which all living elements receive full attention.

For reasons which have to do with the teaching of landscape design in France, specialists in this field are well trained today to deal with space in aesthetic or plastic terms; so much so that their work is often assimilated to artistic creations which, when finished, bear a recognizable signature. Land Art, born of vast American spaces, has had a definite influence on attitudes that treat landscape design as a fine art (from a conceptual point of view) and also on the preference given to form over any other parameter—spatial, temporal or biological.

This pre-eminence of the visual coincides almost always with an architectural bias. It comes as no surprise then to find architects turning to landscape and relegating the choice of living material, of individual species (always considered of secondary importance) to some obscure gardener. It is assumed that the main aim, above all, is to compose a given space, it matters little with what elements.

As for gardeners, in recent decades they have drifted away from being experienced organizers of space towards becoming mere technicians (French municipal gardeners are called *techniciens de surface*). They take charge of 'green spaces' (*espaces vert*), which reduce nature to a kind of comfort, an urban convenience, a smooth décor which can be mowed, pruned, blown, vacuumed, machinated in all possible ways to provide the sterile object which people seem to want now: a foil for urban constructions.

Never, without doubt, has the desire to do what is best for nature been so destructive of its object. Never has life, caught in the hands of developers, been more threatened and subjected to a thousand toxic products that make the garden centres rich. Never has the very vocabulary of gardening become so devoid of meaning. It is surprising, and revealing, to note that a 'treatment' is not today designed to support life but to kill.

Natural science as an aim in itself, apart from merely practical applications, has long since disappeared from any teaching syllabus. The only holdout is a version of biology, an immense field reduced entirely today to macrobiology – the invisible world of genetics.

It is understandable and perhaps even inevitable that professionals who shape space today, having no experience in observing nature much less any ongoing complicity with visible living matter – although they make use of it – have fallen back onto the only elements at their disposal: shapes, colours, textures and smells organized into pictures.

Thus arises the strange and dangerous gap between the world of science and that of the developers. In the current state of scientific discourse, there is a real barrier between those who exert an influence on the environment and those who know what it is made of. This accounts in part for the isolation of ecologists until very recently. This explains also the extreme muddle of some of its adepts (the French 'verts', political formations) who, when no one listens to them and they find no means to pursue their urgent projects, get stuck, purely and simply, in ideological battles.

To approach nature, one must not be a developer but first and foremost a naturalist. A child's awareness is a good starting point; but this sense of wonder, though luckily it does not belong only to childhood, remains associated with it. Critics assume that nothing very serious can emerge from such an emotional link between an individual and his or her environment.

The means used by society to blind and deafen itself to nature's over-pressing requirements are always more or less the same. After dismissing the child in any adult capable of wonder, critics mask the urgency of the environment's needs with a strange cultural smokescreen which we call art. It is enough to say that an ecologist is an artist. Unspoken is the comment: 'It's not serious, he or she will probably outgrow it'.

Thus it is very difficult for anyone dealing with space – a landscape designer for example – to develop an ecological argument as the principal line of reflection in working out a project. If the argument is based on hard science, it is perceived as boring. If it does not refer to hard science, it is filed away in the category of ineffectual poetic exercises.

I proposed for the Parc André Citroën in Paris that the twin pavilions be used to raise insects (*Saturnides lepidoptera* in one, *Trichopters* in the other). This was considered rather baroque, unconnected with the theme of the garden. Of course I had not intended a direct relation to the ecological management of the park as a whole but simply a project that would sensitize the visiting public to this category of fauna and help them learn to observe insects.

The world of insects continues to frighten even people who ordinarily make use of natural space. The role of insects in the ecological chain is not obvious to the clients of landscape designers. As for the manner in which living species can provide clues to biological balance, this is completely unknown to developers and is only just becoming familiar to the general public. These considerations always raise urgent questions about development itself. Yes, the presence of sorrel means acid soil, lichen on the branch of an oak reveals clean air, certain toads indicate water with a good biological balance, the flight of a lacewing confirms an environment free of pesticides, but what can one do with all that?

This apparently innocent question usually brings on the chainsaws, the parade of bulldozers, the round of cement mixers. The state of things as they are before development even begins has no interest whatever for the developers; a project which would consist of doing nothing but respecting the existing balance of a site would get no votes in an election.

For these reasons – and let us say because of the immense and overall resistance to ecology until very recently in France – it serves no purpose to invoke this science (or philosophy) to strengthen the appeal of a project proposal. The best one can hope for is to alert opinion through symbols or practices that may help change the public's attitude towards the environment. By way of example I might cite three attempts at development and management organized around ecological principles that I have been commissioned to create in France:

1. The Deborence Island at the Parc Matisse in Lille, which proposes a piece of nature left to its own devices.

2. The Mediterranean gardens at the Domaine du Rayol in the south, centred on Mediterranean biomes from all over the world, in particular connection to the theme of fire.

3. The Moving Garden of the Parc André Citroën, with its wildflower-filled rough grass, where the management of different parts is done with a view to the evolution of local biodiversity.

But in certain cases, one may ask if humankind's adaptation to nature should involve development at all. It can only be destructive and in that sense particularly archaic when compared to the simple observation of nature, intended to promote understanding before intervention.

For we who are invited to meditate on 'landscape', it is essential to know whether any proposal will be taken seriously that includes – as certain subjects require – large expanses of non-intervention. Is it possible to raise non-intervention and in some cases even the undoing of development to the status of project? And to propose instead a small-scaled educational adventure concerning grass and the beings that live in it: 'microcosmic' marvels revealed as much by technology as by real talent?

How may we save ourselves from lawns and all the other harmful types of comfortable propriety? How can we bring about a future rich enough in tolerance to conceive of spaces where nature collaborates with humankind rather than be seen as an obstacle to our desires? These are the questions that arise when a client (public or private) allows the specialist who will intervene – here a landscape gardener – to approach the site not as a technician or an artist but as a naturalist.

HORTICULTURAL INTERVENTION ART

Tony Heywood

In this essay the author – a garden maker and artist – expounds his vision of an exciting new trend in gardens: the garden as art intervention.

A new approach to garden design is evolving in urban England. At the same time the practice of traditional gardening is alive and well in Britain, though its theoretical side is in a quiet crisis. Much of British garden design is now stagnating under a welter of pastiche, faux ruralism and design solutions. The causes of this crisis are various and most are deep seated, but the signs of it can be seen in the reluctance to accept new ways of looking at the whole concept of gardening and landscaping.

In recent years a new way of designing outdoor space has been slowly developing. This might conveniently be referred to as Horticultural Intervention Art, or HIA. Its repertoire consists of the sort of structures/installations/gardens that can be seen at garden festivals like Westonbirt in England, Chaumont-Sur-Loire in France, Lausanne in Switzerland, and the Jardin de Metis in Canada. These events are generally called something along the lines of a 'Contemporary Garden Festival' and feature gardens like Candace Behouth's , made entirely from plastic. To say such gardens are controversial is to underestimate the issue. In fact they have galvanized more traditional gardeners to transform their ploughshare into swords, so to speak, as a debate at the Royal Horticultural Society's bicentennial in 2004 attested. It ran: 'This House believes that horticultural craft will determine the culture of gardens of the future, at the expense of artistic expression.' The words 'Or else' are not in the motion, though they could be heard emanating from the mouths of speakers who would rather these new styles of gardens weren't considered to be gardens at all but as artworks. The intention of this essay is to ask why these new gardens provoke such heated debate.

THE DOMINANT IDEA IN THE BRITISH TRADITION

Though gardening is often discussed in terms of being the British vernacular art form, the idea of the garden as a form for artistic expression appears to be anathema in many quarters. The garden has fallen from grace as an expression of this artistic impulse. Instead, the focus now centres on the garden's practical, decorative and meditative functions.

The traditional garden clearly is a meditative space, a retreat from the world. And in a twist that is perhaps Western rather than British, these social retreats are not spiritual retreats, though they are thick with ritual. Instead they prioritize the material and functional aspects of gardening. Gardeners, once in their garden, typically strive to suggest they have become removed from any other cultural system. The garden is an island divorced from a wider context.

There is a wilful and often rather admirable determination by many gardeners to have none of the nonsense of modern life. A garden is a refuge from people, fashion and new conceptual ideas. It is a spiritual haven without even a God to get in the way – the open-air manifestation of the man in his shed, the triumph of the practical over the conceptual. Empiricism, in other words.

This is all very well and good, but before the traditional gardener gets too cosy, it needs to be said that it is not empiricism that has repeatedly put British gardens at the forefront of garden design, rather a harnessing and developing of current new strands of thought in a garden context. Westonbirt garden festival may be the perfect spatial laboratory to develop these or put concepts to the test.

The empirical tradition in British thinking values experience over the innovative concept, seeks to put all ideas to the practical test before they can be put into play (notice even the differences between the Westonbirt and the Chaumont garden festivals: the latter clearly pursuing a more cerebral approach). On the plus side, this saves us be-cardiganed British from the wild mistakes of pure theory. On the minus side, it robs us of colour in our thinking. And where would a garden be without colour?

There is another philosophical and social position which is currently stultifying garden design in this country and which is antithetical to new developments. The more extreme exponents of this position see gardens as essentially reactionary/oppositional. A garden's job is to resist culture and promote nature, to deny the urban and glorify the rural (the *rus in urbe* aesthetic), to promote the simple over the contrived, commonsense over thought-through.

What the traditional garden and its many champions are doing here is continuing a trend very evident in the work of many British interior designers. The garden's conceptual job is to promote the upper-class aesthetic at the expense of the middle-class aesthetic.

The upper-class aesthetic affects everything, but does nothing. Everything happens by divine right. The upper-class aesthetic favours casual effortlessness over effort, believes taste is an innate quality rather than something learned and learnable, promotes the arcane processes of breeding rather than the transparentness of education, trusts wisdom rather than book-learning, the natural (picturesque) over the artificial, harmony over disjuncture and clash. Not for nothing are Farrow & Ball or National Trust colour schemes muted, tranquil, and nature-derived.

HORTICULTURAL INTERVENTION ART

Into this world that prizes the rural, the empirical and the upper class comes the new boy: Horticultural Intervention Art (HIA). It is no surprise that HIA hits resistance in many quarters, since it offers neither a godless spiritual retreat, nor an empirical field of experiment, nor a validation of gracious living. In fact it necessarily rejects all of these.

The HIA movement is urban-based and proud of it; takes as its starting point not nature in its organic sense but the media-focused world of popular culture, film and music in which it finds itself; is interested in the artificial; makes no claims to classic status; looks like hard work; and its taste is questionable, even provocative.

Unlike most forms of gardening, HIA takes as both its site and its inspiration the urban landscape – advertising hoarding, window display, the computer screen and other new media. And as with those examples, it requires constant renewal to keep achieving its effect.

These HIA gardens belong in the thrust of urban language where disciplines collapse together into a pool of meaning – on the street one day, on television the next, in the bin the third. This is not to say that these gardens could not become timeless, just that they have no urge to be.

What's more, and here they become of particular interest in a commercial sense, they reject what is often proposed as 'the urban garden' – the vaguely minimalist architect-designed complement to every new building, which relies on lawns, hard-edged design-led solutions and a tastefully chosen piece of sculpture representing, presumably, human scale and involvement. The pubic hair to the architect's grand phallus. The fact that these gardens are not about plants has led to objections from some quarters that they're not gardens at all. Well, nor is a garden of remembrance and that seems to draw no flak. In fact the horticultural installation could claim to be following in the great tradition of garden innovators who drew directly from the cultures they grew out of to create new styles of gardens. As the gardens of Versailles set out to mirror a worldview based on a finely wrought divine plan, so Capability Brown's work was imbued with early notions of Romanticism, which sought to foreground the nobility of nature. All the great garden design innovations have drawn directly from the wider culture. Similarly, HIA draws its inspiration from recent concerns about the defining role of the media, the power of the surface image and the triumph of trivia. These horticultural installations are real gardens – gardens of earthly delights, treasure cabinets, labs of exotica and social spaces.

If, as has been suggested, these works are more artistically driven, this approach to garden landscape perhaps offers a new direction for the art world. It could be likened to process art – where the HI artist actually uses the gardens as a means to solve the problem that he himself deliberately crafted, as opposed to most landscapers who find design solutions for pre-existing problems. In a further development, horticultural-based art introduces notions of participation. This is not just a fanciful idea, as two recent group exhibitions, 'State of Play' at the Serpentine, 2004, and 'Common Wealth' at the Tate, 2003, make plain.

When conceptualization has reduced art to pure theory, coupled with the demonization of the material, and traditional gardening has reduced the garden to a series of over-worked clichés based on empiricism, these Horticultural Interventions will enliven both disciplines.

While these HIA gardens are overtly idea-driven, they often appear physically separate from the space they occupy. They are in a place but they are not of a place. They deny the *genius loci*, sometimes playfully, sometimes wilfully. Because of their apparent lack of functional qualities (more than decorative) one's response may be one of disinterestedness, promoting a sense of psychic distance, a vital pre-condition for an 'aesthetic experience'. We may ask how this affects our appreciation of the site since these gardens clearly open it up to a multitude of readings.

These works may not be indifferent to the place – as in 1960s public art works, which often appear as arrogant corporate statements – but neither are they site dominated. Physically they acknowledge the place – light levels, wind, scale and size – but they do not need to empathize with it or reflect aspects of it. This is landscaping as site-referenced or site-responsive.

This new approach is particularly relevant in an age where we are questioning notions of community and place, where urban development often creates 'non-spaces' (areas under flyovers, inaccessible courtyards, spaces between urban developments and the like). In places like these HIs can create a local identity in an increasingly globally serialized environment.

Because these HIs are overtly idea-driven they have their own internal logic and can be seen, like art works, as things with meaning – 'significant forms'. Language cannot describe them fully, they are their own non-verbal expressive communication systems. Their topography is thick with signifiers, often jostling for attention.

A traditional garden too is full of signifiers. But in these cases the signifiers are attached to an organic form and intent can become overwhelmed (has the gardener used a white flower to suggest purity, or is it just a shade-tolerant, acid lover?). HIs remove all of a garden's conflicting points of discussion and focus attention on its 'significant' conceptual part. A point of controversy.

Of course traditional gardens have 'significance' too. Words and photographs do not describe them fully. But in a broader sense the conflict between traditional gardens and these newer, urban-style gardens might be as much about language as anything else. But there is nothing new here. After all, try describing

Gertrude Jekyll's gardens in the terms of Versailles or Charles Jencks. It's clear that for a gardening practice that is grounded in urban reality, traditional ways of description based on empirical, rural and 'common-sense' notions is not possible. It is also clear we need to develop a new language with which to explain these new installation gardens and which is intelligible to gardeners of all schools.

The HIA garden relies on surface and image. Take for example my own garden design 'Helter Skelter'. This vorticist arrangement of metal and cactus on a windy corner of London's busy Edgware Road clearly challenges the *genius loci*: it is symbolic and metaphorical, and takes as its subject not nature itself but representations of nature. Unsurprisingly, it doesn't yield to analysis based on soil pH, shade tolerance and the like – although correct horticultural principles were adhered to, as in all HIA work.

A language based on adjectives ('big', 'white', 'beautiful', etc.) is inappropriate here. To crack the symbolic nature of such a garden, a tool designed for this sort of work is necessary. Poetics offer a way forwards. And unlike traditional methods of describing gardens, it is relatively baggage-free, at least in this context. Examples might include: oxymoron – contradictory elements inside a single expression, such as Herman de Vries' garden at Munster (chaotic growth inside a formal walled structure); antiphrasis – using material contrary to what is expected, such as Siobhan Hapaska's work 'Land' (in which the plants appear to be growing from a giant aluminium meteorite); meiosis – an understatement using materials that makes something seem less significant than it used to be (as in my own 'Urbo-Edo' where the use of steel origami-based forms enclose the rockscape); cliché and pun (as in Martha Schwartz's 'Bagel Garden' or astro-turf topiaries).

A more poetic description allows gardeners of all persuasions and critics alike to approach and discuss HIA in a refreshing and playful way, close to the spirit of the practitioners of HIA. This avenue of possibility is fruitful because it's adaptable. Traditional gardens deal very much in concepts like oxymoron and antiphrasis, they just don't discuss themselves in such terms. Thus the language of poetics might offer both a starting point for a discussion of these new forms of gardening and an idiom within which traditional and HIA garden designers could speak to each other.

Surely there is room in the garden for everybody?

UNNATURAL HISTORY
Women, Gardening and Femininity

Rozsika Parker

The distinctive yet often hidden role of women in the history of gardening is traced here in terms of gender tension, a tension that is as apparent as ever today.

There is surely nothing gender specific about 'green fingers'. Yet men and women have significantly different histories in the garden. Class and sex have intersected to shape the history of women and gardening in quite particular ways. Despite gender equality in gardening today, traces of the past are evident in women's relationships to gardening and instil gardening practice with a particular sensitivity to issues of gender.

Drawing on contemporary writings on gardening, and focusing upon the emergence of the middle class gardener, I shall map the impact on women of the philosophy and practice of gardening since the sixteenth century. It is a history of restrictions. But in transcending the obstacles confronting them, women gardeners have, to my mind, developed attitudes and practices which today benefit gardening as a whole.

Until the nineteenth century, women did not have the education, the psychological permission or the practical opportunities to write gardening handbooks, hence I shall infer the position of women from the words of men.

In 1557 Thomas Tusser published *A Hundreth good pointes of husbandrie united to as many of good housewifery*, 'For huswifes must husbande, as wel as the man'. Contemporary paintings also give the impression that both men and women, at all levels of society, worked in the gardens. Tusser's title indicates that there was a sexual division of labour, but because the garden provided for both the culinary and medicinal needs of the household, women had particular responsibility for the garden. In 1577 Barnaby Googe in *Four Bookes of Husbandry* declared that 'old husbandes used always to judge that where they founde the Garden out of order, the wife of the house (for unto her belonged the charge thereof) was no good huswyfe'.[1]

By the seventeenth century an even more pronounced gender division is suggested by the publication of a book addressed solely to women: *The Countrie Housewife's Garden* by William Lawson (1618). Nevertheless, women were not yet considered to have a specific emotional relationship with plants or a particular affinity with flowers. John Parkinson, for example, declared that an appreciation of violets denoted a 'liberall and gentlemanly mind', while John Rea in 1695 instructed men to love their plants to make them prosper. Yet a restrictive division of labour had undoubtedly emerged. In 1685 John Evelyn visited Lord and Lady Clarendon's house at Swallowfield in Berkshire and admired the garden: 'My lady being so extraordinarily skilled in the flower, and my Lord in diligence of planting'.[2] William Temple who gardened in partnership with his wife Dorothy Osborne agreed, remarking that 'flowers were more the ladies part than the man's'.[3]

This hardening gender division needs to be understood in the context of anxiety in relation to gender difference during the seventeenth century, arising from the social and ideological upheavals provoked by the rise of Puritanism and the Civil War. Sex-role differentiation was hotly debated in pamphlets with such titles as 'Another Blast Against Manly Women and Effeminate Men'. John Evelyn envisioned a gardening partnership between men and women but with clearly defined rules: 'a Wife cleanses, scrapes and weeds, while the Master and his men labour about harder, more in haste'.[4]

This 'different but equal' partnership came under threat in the early years of the eighteenth century with the changing status of gardens and gardening. With the rise of the middle class, the possession of both a fine garden and a dependent lady came to signify a man's social standing. This fostered both the professionalization of gardening and the marginalization of women gardeners. A wife maintained her husband's position by a style of living and a mode of behaviour associated with the aristocratic lady, and characterized by an absolute absence of all visible work except embroidery. 'What a delightful entertainment it must be to the fair sex, whom their native modesty, and the tenderness of men towards them, exempts from publick business, to pass their time in imitating fruit and flowers, and transplanting all the beauties of nature into their own dress or raising a new creation in their closets', Addison commented in the *Spectator* in 1716.[5]

Women were not precisely forbidden the garden but their activities were restricted. In his book *The Ladies Recreation or The Art of Gardening* (1719), Charles Evelyn observed that, 'The management of the Flower Garden in particular is oftentimes the Diversion of the ladies where the Gardens are not very extensive, and the Inspection thereof doth not take up too much of their Time'.[6] The garden had become a lady's diversion.

From its inception, the eighteenth-century concept of femininity, which mirrored the attributes of the aristocratic lady, aroused consternation. Critiques of women's behaviour – inculcated though deemed innate – came from every shade of opinion, from medical textbooks, to conduct literature and from political tracts to gardening handbooks. In *A New System of Agriculture* (1726), John Lawrence commented, 'If inclination and leisure could but once agree and unite, I flatter myself the Ladies would soon think that their vacant Hours in the Culture of the Flower-Garden, would be more innocently spent and with greater Satisfaction than the common Talk over a Tea-Table where Envy and Detraction so commonly preside'.[7]

Stephen Switzer, in *The Nobleman, Gentleman and Gardeners Recreation*, also offers gardening as a lifeline to ladies but in language that reveals the lady's distance from the practice: 'When men are observed to busie themselves in this diverting and useful Employ, 'tis no more than what is from them expected; but when by the fair and Delicate sex, it has something in it that looks supernatural, something so much above the trifling amusements of Ladies'. [8]

A shift in the philosophy and practice of gardening by the mid-eighteenth century transformed the image of the lady in the garden from supernatural to eminently natural. Women's relation to gardening was determined by the evolving idealization of nature. Among theorists of the Enlightenment, the intellectual movement that dominated Europe and America for much of eighteenth century, Rousseau gave clearest expression to the values associated with bourgeois femininity. His description of an ideal girl's upbringing was serialized in the *Ladies Magazine* in 1762. In his novel *La Nouvelle Heloise* (1761), 'Julie's Garden' appeared as if fashioned by nature alone. Love of nature was considered innate to women and evidence of both piety and purity. A lady in a garden was viewed simply as one flower amongst many.

Knowledge of botany and botanical embroidery were the sanctioned expressions of the lady's oneness with nature. Surviving letters indicate that embroidery and gardening could and did go hand in hand. Mary Delany, a famed botanical embroiderer, wrote to her sister: 'You think, madam, I have no garden perhaps. But that's a mistake: I have one as big as your parlour at Gloucester, and in it groweth damask-roses, stocks variegated and plain, some purple, some red, Pinks, Philaria, some dead and some alive; and honeysuckles that never blow. But when you come to town to weed and water, it shall be improved after the new taste, but till then it shall remain dishevelled and undressed'. [9]

Despite the growing insistence that ladies were too frail and delicate to garden, it seems that they continued to be involved in horticulture, although as weeders and waterers. The elision between women and gardens is evident in Delany's description of the garden as 'dishevelled and undressed'.

The identification of women with nature and flowers set the scene for women's formal entry into gardening practice in the nineteenth century. The femininity that was considered to have rendered ladies too frail to garden was now taken as evidence of a natural proclivity for gardening. Women were the natural gardeners for the gardens surrounding the new suburban villas. The domain of 'the angel in the house' extended into the garden, where a woman was expected to demonstrate her moral goodness and her worth as a wife by the neatness, orderliness and health of her flower-beds.

At the same time, an improvement in women's education led to the appearance of the first books on gardening by women, with Lady Charlotte Murray's *British Gardens* (1799), Marie E. Jackson's *Botanical Dialogues – Designed for the Use of Schools* (1797) and Mrs Henriette Moriarty's *Viridarium or Green House Plants* (1806). Soon the Victorian doctrine of separate spheres fostered a renewed gender division in garden writing, with books designed specifically for three groups: gentlemen, children and ladies. The writer and gardener who transformed the face of female gardening was Jane Loudon. A Gothic and science fiction novelist, she married the gardener–journalist John Claudius Loudon in 1830. When his right arm was amputated, she gardened for him and transcribed the texts of his books. After his death, assisted by her daughter Agnes, she became an enormously successful and prolific writer of thoughtful, comprehensive books and magazine articles on gardening. Her first book, *Gardening for Ladies* (1843), challenged the received wisdom that ladies were too delicate to dig, for 'no lady is likely to become fond of gardening who does not do a great deal with her own hands'. Chapter one, 'Stirring the Soil', instructed women how to dig without unsexing themselves: 'It must be confessed that digging appears at first sight a very laborious employment, and one peculiarly unfitted to small and delicately formed hands and feet, but by a little attention to the principles of mechanics and the laws of motion, the labour may be much simplified and rendered easy'.[10]

Jane Loudon was writing at the time of a recodification of ideas about women, stirred by the often-contradictory ethics of industrialization, evangelism and political radicalism. Whereas eighteenth-century femininity was equated with not working, by the time Jane Loudon published, the feminine ideal consisted in working hard for love of God, the family and the home. As we have seen, eighteenth-century writers, concerned that the construction of femininity produced decadent ladies, advocated an interest in gardening for ladies. Jane Loudon, on the other hand, recognized that the construction of femininity led not to decadence but depression. Aware of the cost to women of the doctrine of separate spheres, of the loneliness and frustration entailed, she wrote *The Ladies Country Companion: How to Enjoy a Country Life Rationally* (1845). In a series of letters addressed to an isolated, newly married woman, she advocates gardening as therapy: 'Gardening is one of those happy arts in which there is always some not quite certain change to look forward to, and to be anxious about'.[11]

Despite the changes that Jane Loudon's writing both illustrated and initiated, she was careful to maintain the signs of feminine respectability within the doctrine of separate spheres. She introduces her first book with the words, 'When I married Mr Loudon, it is scarcely possible to imagine a person more completely ignorant than I.' Well into the twentieth century women garden writers continued to represent themselves as ignorant amateurs. Alicia Amhurst prefaces the first history of gardening with a declaration of her own inadequacy and indebtedness to

Mr Percy Newberry. Marion Cran, writing in the 1920s, reassures readers of *The Garden of Experience* that her previous publication was entitled *The Garden of Ignorance*. Gertrude Jekyll describes herself as a 'practical amateur'.

By 1900, however, with emerging feminism and the rise of the Suffrage Movement, the doctrine of separate spheres became not the basis for subordination but a source of strength for women, from which to demand equal rights and professional possibilities. Women began to organize together as gardeners. In 1899 the Women's Agricultural and Horticultural International Union was formed and by 1910 had 250 members. As Judith Condon and Anne Jennings have argued, the entry of women professionally changed the face of gardening: 'Gardening was a working-class trade. Most boys who trained to be gardeners were apprenticed. Those who championed women into horticulture believed gardening should be approached as a "profession". The lady gardener would be from a middle-class background and college trained.'[12] By 1900, a girl wishing to study horticulture had a choice of three colleges: Swanley, Studley and Reading. Two world wars confirmed women in their role as gardeners and today women are professionally active in all areas of horticulture.

This necessarily schematic overview of some 300 years of women's gardening history indicates the extent to which women's role in gardening was shaped by changing notions of femininity. A woman's garden and her gardening became a measure of her morality, purity and spirituality, and also a means of self-improvement. Hence a strong vein of morality has flourished amongst women gardeners. 'I always think of my sins when I weed', writes Helena Rutherford Ely, 'They grow apace in the same way and are harder still to get rid of.' She titled her book *A Woman's Hardy Garden*. (By 1900 ladies had given way to women.) Gardening provided an opportunity to practise the virtue of hard work with and on behalf of the Lord's creation.

The high moral tone of the woman gardener was magnified by the involvement of gardening with the ideals of the Arts and Crafts Movement, embodied in Gertrude Jekyll: 'It is better to me to deny myself the pleasure of having it, than to evidence the mild sense of guilt of having placed it where it neither does itself justice nor accords with its neighbours, and where it reproaches me every time I pass it'.[13] Fifty-three years later, a comparable moral note sounds in the writings of Vita Sackville-West: 'One says also to oneself, "Have I done the best I could with this responsibility which I took on"'.[14] Women, with a history of 'high-minded gardening', have been well prepared for the eco-consciousness increasingly evident amongst gardeners today.

A woman and her garden have been viewed not only as living proof of her morality but as an extension of her being and above all of her biology. A woman's body has been seen to dictate her ability or disability as a gardener. The legacy is a tendency to experience the garden as an extension of the self – specifically the body. Jill Cowley, for example, writing in 1987 observes, 'I find I am sympathetic to giant plants, probably because I am rather big myself'.[15] Would a man confess to a penchant for Alpines on account of his stature?

The source of women's identification with plants is, of course, the elision of women and nature. I think this has fostered a particular relationship to plants. Jill Cowley describes herself as 'sympathetic' to plants. Whereas both men and women personify plants, I would suggest that women also project their feelings into plants. Take, for example, William and Dorothy Wordsworth – both gardeners, both of whom wrote of the daffodils they encountered on a walk. William personified the dancing, jocund daffodils and was cheered by their recollection in tranquillity. Dorothy attributed greater psychological complexity and diversity to the daffodils: 'some rested their heads upon these stones, as on a pillow for weariness, and the rest tossed and reeled, and danced, and seemed as if they verily laughed'.[16]

Empathy with plants heightens the experience of gardening. Women gardeners describe suffering on behalf of their plants. Cutting back, pruning, lifting and dividing are felt to be acts of cruelty. Margery Fish, for example, writes of the bugle, 'It always looks at home and when I find it trespassing it goes to my heart to have to fork it out and I am glad when I can find a good home for the poor unsuspecting creature'.[17]

Others glory in the sanctioned aggression, otherwise outlawed by the construction of femininity. Indeed, part of the pleasure of gardening for women has been the permission it provided to transgress the bounds of femininity. The aggressive physicality of gardening has carried particular meaning for women. In 1898 Elizabeth von Arnim writes how she 'literally ache[s] with envy as [she] watch[es] the men going about their pleasant work in the sunshine, turning up the luscious damp earth'.[18] She describes slinking out with a spade and rake, and feverishly digging before running back into the house, hot and guilty, and getting into a chair and behind a book, looking languid just in time to save her reputation. Pleasure in physical labour continued to be expressed by women gardeners throughout the twentieth century. 'There is no sport in the world that compares with clearing bindweed', declared Margery Fish.[19] Male gardeners in comparable circumstances sound a similar note. Monty Don, for example, deprived of manual labour by his success as a media gardener, confesses, 'I like to get tired and sweaty and dirty, and often envy the people I pay to do that for me.'[20]

To gain an understanding of women's position as gardeners, we need to piece together the history of gardening with the social history of women. For example, the synthesis of self and garden, coupled with a restricted opportunity for autobiographical writing, led women to develop the genre of autobiographical garden writing. Elizabeth von Arnim published *Elizabeth and her German Garden* to great acclaim in 1898. At the same time more practical works by women included entire chapters of autobiography. In *Home and Garden: Notes and Thoughts Practical and Critical, of a Worker in Both*, Gertrude Jekyll has a chapter called 'Home Pussies' in which she describes her cats and her ability to distinguish their different purrs in the dark. Elizabeth von Arnim's writing had a huge impact on Miriam Rothschild who complemented her scientific, entomological writing with lyrical, autobiographical accounts of her commitment to wildflower gardening. Today the genre has been taken up by men. One of many, Monty Don writes an engagingly autobiographical column, 'My Roots' in the *Observer*. Coincidentally, the day I finished this essay, he published a celebration of his gardening partnership with his wife.[21] He attributes their contrasting approaches to innate gender difference. I am suggesting that whatever differences there may or may not be between male and female gardeners, they are at present historically and culturally determined.

In addition to gardening in partnership, friendship has been of great importance to gardening women. Reading women's accounts of their gardening, it becomes clear that friendship plays a crucial part in their enjoyment of gardening. Nancie Sheffield is typical in the importance she accords cuttings from friends: 'I can never feel lonely, as so many of my friends have given me plants and I feel as if they are almost there in the garden with me'.[22] Given their restricted access to art practices understood to be pursued only by the 'isolated genius', women have long been associated with collective art practices – for example quilting – pursued for love, not money, and fuelled by friendship. The spirit of those arts has carried over into gardening.

The elision of women with nature in the eighteenth century coincided with an idealization of motherhood. By the mid-nineteenth century both gardening and motherhood were seen as coming naturally to all women, and a staple subject of embroidered pictures was a mother and child enclosed together in the

garden. In the twentieth century, owning up to maternal ambiva-
lence, women admitted that far from being contiguous with
motherhood, gardening provided a welcome relief from the exi-
gencies of childcare. Anthea Gibson, for example, comments
that for the middle-aged woman gardener 'it is a relief to be free
from the tyranny of the sand-pit'.[23] Of course there are links
between gardening and childcare: both evoke the desire to control the uncontrollable, along with passionate love, impatience
and guilt. But plants stay in place while children struggle to separate. The journalist Jill Tweedie remarked ironically, 'Having
children is preparation for gardening.'

We are now at a particularly interesting juncture in terms of
gender and gardening. Androgyny is being both promoted and
resisted. Commercial interests maintain a gender division by
addressing women gardeners as a separate consumer group.
Hence a mail-order catalogue advertises, 'A moisturising cream
designed to revive hands that have been busy weeding, pruning
and tidying.' At the same time, women's magazines continue the
tradition of the garden as an extension of a woman's self, with
features entitled 'Must-Have-Plants', which represent the garden as a fashion accoutrement. Book titles continue to appear
along gender lines, for example, *A Man's Turf: The Perfect Lawn*
(2000) by Warren Schultz and Roger Foley, followed by *A Man's
Garden* (2001) by Warren Schultz. It seems as if gardening has
become so imbued with notions of femininity that masculinity
needs to be emphasized.

Despite the long history of gender division in the garden,
there are signs of change, as is evident in one of the main public
faces of gardens – media gardening. Unlike Percy Thrower,
today's male television gardeners more often than not work in
partnership with a female gardener: Alan Titchmarsh worked
with Charlie Dimmock, who demonstrated that hard landscaping was by no means the prerogative of the male gardener.
Nevertheless, the camera lingered on her body and long hair,

hinting at bra-lessness, emphasizing the exceptional nature of
her achievement and maintaining the elision between woman
and the natural. Though manifesting an 'unfeminine' muscular-
ity, she was preserved for the feminine gardening stereotype.
Rachel de Thame, who has worked with Monty Don and Joe
Swift, amongst others, is demonstrably knowledgeable in all
aspects of gardening, yet her personal slot in the television programme *Gardeners' World* was called 'Rachel's Flower Hour'.
Monty Don assured viewers that male gardeners were equally
adept in the flower garden; nevertheless I was forcibly reminded
of Lady Clarendon, who, in the seventeenth century, was 'so
extraordinarily skilled in the flower'. As well as working alongside women, male presenters evince a new creative emotionality
in the face of flowers, an emotionality hitherto associated with
women. However, they buttress their masculine identity with
planes, helicopters and off-road vehicles, as, for example, in
Chris Beardshaw's television programme *The Flying Gardener*,
recalling Edward Budding's reflection on his invention of the
lawnmower in 1832: 'Country gentlemen may find, in using my
machine themselves, an amusing, useful and healthy exercise.'

I have delineated ways that gender tension has structured the
history of gardening. At different historical moments it has fostered a division of labour that is oppressive and restrictive to
women. But women have challenged and transcended the obstacles they faced and, to my mind, the particular psychological
attributes instilled in women today generally enrich the practice
of gardening.

NOTES

1. Cited in Eleanour Sinclair Rohde, *The Old-World Pleasaunce*, London, 1925, p. 99.

2. Cited in Rozsika Parker, *The Subversive Stitch: Embroidery and the Making of the Feminine*, London, 1984, p. 95.

3. Cited in Jane Fearnley-Whittingstall, *The Garden: An English Love Affair*, London, 2002.

4. Cited in Sinclair Rohde, p.100.

5. Cited in Parker, p. 114.

6. Cited in Sinclair Rohde, p.101.

7. Cited in *ibid.*, p.102.

8. Cited in *ibid.*, p.104.

9. Cited in Fearnley-Whittingstall, p.162.

10. Cited in Jane Loudon, *Gardening for Ladies*, London, 1843, p. 6.

11. Cited in Thomasina Beck, *Embroidered Gardens*, London, 1979, p. 101.

12. J. Condon and A. Jennings, *Women Gardeners*, The Museum of Garden History.

13. Cited in Deborah Kellaway (ed.), *The Virago Book of Women Gardeners*, London, 1995, p. 84.

14. Cited in *ibid.*, p. 241.

15. Cited in Alvilde Lees-Milne and Rosemary Verey (eds), *The New Englishwoman's Garden*, London, 1987, p. 61.

16. Cited in Kellaway (ed.), p.120.

17. Cited in *ibid.*, p.54)

18. Elizabeth von Arnim, *The Solitary Summer* (first published 1899), London, 1993, p. 14.

19. Cited in Kellaway (ed.), p. 15.

20. Monty Don, 'My Roots' *Observer Magazine*, 11 January 2004.

21. *Ibid.*, 15 February 2004.

22. Cited in Lees-Milne and Verey (eds), p. 73.

23. Cited in *ibid.*, p. 103.

AS THE GARDEN SO THE EARTH
The Politics of the 'Natural Garden'

Noël Kingsbury

The idea of the 'natural garden' is heavily laden with a burden of political ideology that can get in the way of effectively managing gardens and landscape for sustainability and bio-diversity. The author argues that our relationship with nature will benefit from Enlightenment values rather than what he dubs 'neo-romantic' ones.

The 'natural garden' – a contradiction in terms, some might argue. Surely the whole point of a garden is that it is unnatural, a space organized and ordered by human will? Here I would like to look at this apparent contradiction, at the variety of motivations and ideals behind so-called natural gardens, and the way they refer to the relationship between humanity and nature. In particular I want to look at the natural garden in the light of the ongoing and contested legacy of the Enlightenment. I would argue that the creation and management of natural gardens could be based on either pragmatism and science (i.e. the legacy of the Enlightenment), or on mysticism and ideology, the legacy of the Romantics who from the eighteenth century onwards have criticized and reacted against the Enlightenment. I will go on to argue that it is only the former approach – that is, one based on science – that can really be justified.

Gardens that claim to be 'natural' or 'wild' are nothing new: think of eighteenth-century landscape parks or William Robinson's wild garden. But, with the possible exception of the English landscape garden tradition of the eighteenth century, interest in natural or nature-inspired gardening has never been as intense as it is now. The reasons are not difficult to understand. Those who live in industrialized countries can afford to feel that their civilization has become so alienated from nature that they can indulge a wish to recreate it on their own doorsteps. This is a feature of the post-industrial society; it is difficult to imagine the newly rich middle classes of India or Brazil wanting to create wild gardens.

I would argue that there are, broadly speaking, two groups of motivations behind the desire to create nature-inspired gardens. One could be called naturalist, i.e. the natural history enthusiast or nature lover who wants wildlife on their doorstep and a closer integration with wild places. The naturalist approach is quasi-scientific, growing out of a tradition of the empirical observation of nature, and is engaged at some level with scientific ecology. The second is what I would call neo-romantic, which includes those who are essentially critical of the modern world and feel that we need to reconnect to 'traditional' ways of doing things. Many of those who have pioneered the natural garden style, or are involved in habitat creation professionally, fall into the first camp, yet many of those who now garden 'naturally', or who promote it as part of a media and consumer industry-led 'natural' or 'organic' lifestyle are part of the second. Whether one uses Roundup™ or not seems almost like the shibboleth for either camp. Those in the first category are essentially pragmatic, and will occasionally reach for the weedkiller (generally when starting out with a weed-choked new garden), whereas the second group regard it with unalloyed horror.

DEFINITIONS

One might argue that the only natural garden is one where the owner did nothing, allowing the forces of nature to take over entirely, or where the very definition of 'garden' simply means an enclosure or declaration of a wild area as one's personal property. The result of abandoning a conventional garden, however, will usually be several decades of scrubby weedy chaos as a variety of opportunist plant species establish themselves, before a more stable woodland community becomes a more permanent feature. So-called natural gardening is in fact nothing of the sort, and nobody (except perhaps a few anarchists) seriously suggests that this is any sort of gardening. Instead, natural gardening means different things to different people. To North Americans it can mean informal gardening where shrubs are not clipped, and where sinuous shapes replace straight lines. Such a style is a clear reaction against the classical European heritage of formality, which is often seen reinterpreted in the United States, and against the heavy-handed, indeed almost manic, clipping of evergreens that is part of US popular garden culture. For Europeans it can mean either the creation of plant communities inspired by natural ecosystems, frequently using only native species, or it means the same as organic – this latter usage also being common in North America. An example of this usage is *The Natural Garden*, by Rosamund Richardson,[1] which represents the idea that 'natural' equals 'traditional', with a compilation of traditional gardening methods and wisdom, and rather more recent New Age or organic-sector approaches, including such topics as companion planting – a classic example of the neo-romantic approach.

Here I shall use 'natural' to describe a style that is inspired by the ecology and the aesthetics of natural plant communities.[2]

So, whatever the exact nature of a particular natural garden, it is almost inevitably managed in some way; in other words it is still a cultural artefact. It is useful to think of a gradient between completely formal gardens and unmanaged wildness, with most gardens somewhere on the first part of the gradient; natural gardens are shifted somewhat further on towards the wild. The degree and character of wildness is heavily culturally defined. Plants may be given a relatively free hand in where they can self-seed, but only certain species will be welcome. The species chosen and the overall character of the garden is determined largely by the desire to replicate or evoke particular habitats, ones with a high degree of aesthetic interest, or a range of species which are rated highly for one reason or another. A natural garden is then, the site for an intimate and subtle direction of the natural by the cultural.

NEO-ROMANTIC MYTHOLOGIES

Belief systems are guides to practice, to how one operates in the real world. I believe that the environmental movement (and by extension the natural garden movement) has a choice between following a scientifically based path, informed and inspired by a love of nature (and humanity too, an emphasis not always shared by environmentalists), or a neo-romantic one. Different approaches to natural gardens reflect these ideas in microcosm. In the garden, neo-romantics prefer to be organic, and often espouse the growing of 'native' plants, or 'heritage' plant varieties. Neo-romantic writings about gardens often include references to past ways of living and farming, usually suffused with a hazy golden glow, a good example being Pam Lewis's *Making Wildflower Meadows*.[3] Idealizing the lives and gardens of the poor, or our ancestors, or those in other less advanced cultures, has always been part of the romantic world-view.

Neo-romanticism is an almost officially sanctioned opposition to the apparent hegemony of global capitalism. Neo-romantics are deeply suspicious of science, sceptical about globalization, and have a belief system that is heavily influenced by the New Age and the environmental movements. Amongst the latter, the Deep Ecology movement represents a clearly articulated ideological pole, with a key belief being that the human race has no more rights than any other species, including a denial of any stewardship role.[4] In particular there is an idealization of the relationship between pre-industrial peoples (especially tribal ones) and nature. With support from the Prince of Wales and many other (often wealthy) elite patrons, neo-romanticism offers a safe channel of apparent rebellion against crass modernity. I say 'safe' because it does little to actually challenge economic and political sources of power.

All of us who are critical of the current social, economic and political order imagine how things could be different in the future. However, neo-romantics have a strong tendency to imagine the past having been better than it was, and in many ways better than the present. One of the myths of contemporary neo-romantics is a revival of an old favourite, the noble savage. Tribal, and by extension non-European, and often by further extension, all pre-industrial peoples, are regarded as being good stewards of nature, respecting the animals they kill, the plants they harvest, indeed worshipping nature as a god. Tribal people in particular are regarded as having lived in harmony with an unspoilt nature. This myth has been comprehensively demolished by a number of authors, who have shown that whilst some tribal peoples were good stewards of nature, many have been very destructive of their environments. The Maoris driving all species of the moa bird to extinction within a couple of centuries is merely one example amongst many.[5]

In fact evidence is accumulating that many such peoples manipulated and managed their environments on a huge scale, for example by burning vast tracts of forest on a regular basis to encourage prairie- or savannah-type environments that were a better habitat for game. Biodiversity in some places appears to have suffered, but in others has almost certainly been improved. Whatever, the important point to realize is that many supposedly natural or pristine habitats are nothing of the sort. Even the great Amazonian rainforest may have had its species composition heavily managed by now-extinct groups of Indians.[6]

An example of the complex relationship between human management and nature is to be observed throughout Europe, with the advance of forest over many areas that until recently were grazed as part of a pastoral economy, resulting in the loss of valuable biodiverse and flower-rich meadows. Just as leaving a garden to grow wild does not make a natural garden, so leaving nature to get on with it does not necessarily benefit biodiversity.

SO WHAT IS NATURAL?

After learning about the complex and large-scale interactions between our pre-industrial ancestors and their environments, we have to question the neo-romantic assumption of a pure and untrammelled nature, as set apart from human culture. The two are immeasurably more intertwined than we imagined. Indeed, when faced with environments that are not purely natural but whose biodiversity is the result of a long history of human management, we are confronted with something that cannot possibly be called simply nature, and since these environments cover vastly more of the globe than we have been used to thinking, we are forced to question any neat division between the natural and the cultural. The more we look at the interaction between humanity and the natural environment, the more we appreciate that what we have often thought of as nature is in fact a subtle blend of nature *and* culture – in other words the world looks increasingly like a garden.

'Natural' is a key word in the neo-romantic vocabulary. It is also a key word in the corporate sector that has arisen on the back of neo-romanticism, as more and more companies try to market their goods to this growing, and affluent, body of consumers. While in some cases the word retains real meaning, as in the use of biological controls for insect pests, in many others it does not. The fact that something is 'natural' does not make it any safer (nature is full of poisons), or even more environmentally sound (burning PVC apparently releases fewer dioxins than a bonfire).

Most worrying about the elevation of the word 'natural' is its

elision with essentialism, the belief that human cultures are
determined either by heredity or are in some other way linked
indissolubly to the ethnic group or their physical environment.
Historically environmentalists have been on the illiberal right as
much as the liberal left, and whilst the democratic and multi-
culturalist credentials of most contemporary environmentalists
are not in doubt, there is no clear line between some of the
thinking that comes under the banner of the Deep Ecology
movement or Bioregionalism. Contemporary German far-right
ecologists, for example, make great use of the supposedly natural links between ethnic groups and their environment, effectively denying the fluid, eclectic, evolutionary and dynamic
nature of human cultures. The Nazis were, not surprisingly, hostile to non-native plants, but also adopted an organic agriculture
policy. Their regime stands as a terrible example of what happens when romantic notions of the links between soil and blood
(i.e. genes) get taken to extremes.[7]

NEO-ROMANTICS AND THE LEGACY OF THE ENLIGHTENMENT

The Enlightenment of the eighteenth century was a crucial
breakthrough in human history; the idea that reason should
replace faith as the guide to human action was revolutionary.
Intimately tied up with other major changes: the scientific revolution, the origins of capitalism, the rise of democracy, the
industrial revolution, it marked a fundamental and qualitative
change in the outlook of those societies that have embraced its
values.

At the core of neo-romanticism is a revisionist approach to
the Enlightenment, and its associated revolutions. Many neo-
romantic writers blame it, and the attitudes it fostered, for a
whole raft of the world's ills, particularly those that affect our
relationship with nature. Meanwhile, both the chief proponents
and the popular culture of neo-romanticism place on a pedestal

the supposedly benign and 'holistic' attitudes of pre-Enlightenment societies. The 'primitive' is embraced, tribal peoples celebrated, 'traditional' medicines promoted, 'natural' therapies and solutions marketed. Important figures in the development of science in particular are held responsible for the despoliation of nature, with Francis Bacon and Isaac Newton heading the list of culprits. Lewis Mumford, Kirkpatrick Sale and Rupert Sheldrake are amongst those who hold Enlightenment and early scientific figures responsible for most (if not all) the sins of the modern world.[8]

Whilst the people of the world are clearly better off than ever before, nature has obviously suffered devastation, with post-Enlightenment societies undeniably greatly increasing the rate of destruction started by our remote ancestors. Yet it is part of the legacy of the Enlightenment that we have any concept of the environment, or that other species have rights. The first time that an organized nature conservation movement arrived in history was in the nineteenth century in the United States, a country with not only an enormous amount of 'nature' (so divested of its native peoples that no-one realized that much of the wilderness was in fact managed), but also a climate of opinion arguably more directly derived from Enlightenment thought than any other. Taming nature and making her productive was a large part of Enlightenment thinking, but it was only when the human race ceased to fear nature as a source of trial and tempest, that we could afford to look upon her more benignly.

It should be no surprise then that natural gardens and landscapes appear for the first time too in the age of Enlightenment, with Capability Brown and others. As Enlightenment ideas spread through Europe so does the English landscape garden, with the most spectacular example being Park Wörlitz, in Germany, created by Prince Franz von Anhalt-Dessau, who combined an Enlightenment landscape with religious toleration (including a synagogue), universal education and a welfare system. While today we might argue that it is rather more tame than wild, there is no denying that the English landscape garden marks a fundamental shift in garden history, away from the anthropocentric view of formal garden styles, which viewed nature as only beautiful when ordered by the hand of man. With the Enlightenment arrives the idea that nature itself can be beautiful. Some sort of a role for the wild garden appears earlier though, from none other than the hand of Bacon, *bête noire* of the neo-romantics, in whose essay 'Of Gardens', which describes an ideal garden, there appears a good-sized chunk of wildflower meadow.[9]

GARDENS AND THE STEWARDSHIP OF NATURE

Within the environmental movement there is a wide range of opinions on where the human race stands in relation to the rest of the living world. Broadly speaking, there are two major strands of thinking: the idea of human stewardship over nature; and a denial that the human race has any more rights than any other species. The former view has its roots in Christian tradition, while the latter is argued by the Deep Ecology movement.

Whichever of these standpoints one agrees with, the situation that the human race dominates the earth is undeniable – so as a result, we have stewardship. Whether we deserve it is neither here nor there. Anyone who values the living world will clearly want the human race to exercise its stewardship as responsibly as possible, in particular to mitigate the damage it has done. One way in which this can be done is to create spaces for nature. Our own backyards are a good place to start, and since we will want them to be visually and emotionally pleasing places, a compromise between natural processes and human order seems reasonable.

But should the natural garden be organic? Should it contain only locally native species? These are two issues that are used by some to define a natural garden, and they are questions that might take further essays to answer. Briefly though, a case for pragmatism might be made. A good measure of how well a garden benefits the living world might be how great a measure of biodiversity it supports. Neither organic methods nor a natives-only policy guarantee a higher level of biodiversity, indeed if either allowed particularly aggressive species to flourish, they would actually be detrimental to biodiversity. This requires the application of scientific ecology, if only at a very basic level, that of making observations and collecting – the core activities of the naturalist tradition, which itself was a product of the Enlightenment. The taking of decisions that are based on evidence is the only way to help us reach the goal of higher biodiversity in gardens and the other landscapes we manage, in our role as stewards of nature. On occasion this may mean reaching for the Roundup™. In contrast the neo-romantics would have us attempt to manage using only 'natural' methods, but it is they who define what is natural and what isn't, and those definitions are rooted in misty ideology, and rose-tinted images of how things used to be. At the moment, they say that using a biodegradable herbicide is not 'natural', but that smothering weeds with black plastic or digging them up with a spade is – this distinction is based not on an objective audit of the possible environmental damage caused by either method, but essentially on a faith and ideology, part of which is the belief that synthetic chemicals are all bad.

Sensitive management by a caring human, the gardener, unencumbered by romantic myths and dogmas, informed by empirical observation and science, is the best way forward for garden biodiversity. This sounds like just the recipe for good stewardship of the planet too. As the garden so the earth.

NOTES

1. Rosamund Richardson, *The Natural Garden*, London. 2001.

2. For more details, see Noël Kingsbury, *The New Perennial Garden*, London. 1996.

3. Pam Lewis, *Making Wildflower Meadows*, London. 2003.

4. For a thorough presentation of the movement's ideas see George Sessions, (ed.), *Deep Ecology for the 21st Century*, Boston. 1995.

5. For a discussion of these issues see Peter Coates, *Nature*, Cambridge. 1988, and Martin Lewis, *Green Delusions*, Durham, North Carolina. 1994.

6. See '1491' in *The Atlantic*, March 2002, www.theatlantic.com.

7. See essays by Joachim Wolschke-Bulmahn and Gert Gröning in *Nature and Ideology*, Washington D.C.. 1997.

8. Discussed in Peter Coates, *Nature*, Cambridge. 1988.

9. Discussed in *ibid.*

THE SPIRIT OF THE GEOMETRICIAN

Fernando Caruncho

The celebrated Madrid-based garden designer – or gardener, as he prefers to describe himself – here outlines for the first time in English his personal and poetic philosophy of gardens, inspired by his readings of the Ancients and discovery of geometry.

This essay concerns the diverse analogies between gardens and the visual arts. It deals with the literary and philosophical background that constitutes the garden, both in the West and in the East – its background scenery.

From my point of view, as a gardener, I consider the garden fundamentally as a spiritual and cognitive experience. What I mean by this, is that the growth and development of the emotions within a garden, as well as our knowledge of it, is similar to the effect of a mirror, which reflects from the outside to the inside and from the inside to the outside. On both sides of the mirror there is a garden, and neither side could exist without the mutual reflection of light.

A garden cannot exist for us unless we also evolve an idea of the garden within ourselves, an idea that has been developed at the heart of our cognitive thought. No garden can exist without an interior visualization of a kind that is similar to our imagining of an ideal painting, or of a poem that emerges with the same rhythm as Chinese calligraphy.

This initial process – a product of different emotional states, a mixture of intuitions and memory, of rhythms and rituals learnt and repeated in childhood – constitutes the first stage of the mysterious course of creation. It is a state that is learnt from nature and is lived in solitude or in love, during those years in one's life when innocence opens every door and allows us to see from the highest window of the attic what we will be able to reach in maturity. This is why childhood is sacred: in it, we can intuit what we will be able to achieve, like David with his sling, perhaps. Childhood is the world flowing, the world in action; it is the river that carries us; it is existence opening up and flourishing. What we today call maturity is actually the fulfilment of those visions together with the absence of pain and of loss.

We are constantly repeating rhythms and rituals – in this sense you will not find novelty in my words. I can only try and make you remember part of a common prayer, part of a common heritage that has been forgotten and in which we will find comfort and renewed enthusiasm for the future.

Recalling Malraux, 'The 21st century will be a world of the garden, that is, a spiritual world. Or it won't be', I am a geometrician; I inherit the culture of the Babylonians, the Egyptians and the Persians. They were men who lived in the orchard next to the river, who measured their wheat fields, their vegetable gardens, their reservoirs and, most importantly, the level of the river – all with the help of the geometry of the pyramid.

I discovered the garden – that is, I became conscious of what its idea represented – when I was twenty-one years old, while I was studying philosophy at the University of Madrid. I was then, of course, a young man, seeking the stream that would lead me into the river of life. I was a young apprentice who had never done anything but read chivalric novels and who, obviously, had his head full of the wildest and most fantastic dreams. I could find no better occupation than the study of philosophy. But I was confronted with a paradox: tangled in logic, in the history of science, in epistemology, in metaphysics and in the history of thought, I realized the appalling, cold ruin that our times represented and that, of course, I was a part of. I considered giving up the course, but persisted because in the second year at university our new professor introduced us to Ancient Greece and, with a seminar on Euripides, to classical philosophy.

I then understood that there was nothing more moving than to hunt for the 'hare idea', as the poet José Bergamín would say, and that nothing was more beautiful and horrific than to find yourself in the labyrinthine and abundant forest of thought, under the enigmatic gaze of a deer that looks at you fixedly in an instant that lasts forever and that suspends time.

In this class I began to understand the mythical and symbolic nature of man and how man's dreams are always related to the delightful years of early childhood and youth in Greece, where we, the Indo-Europeans, have our homeland. Thinking back to my childhood and returning to my youth, I was transformed forever into ancient man.

I understood that this master had helped me to remember that we were all 2,700 years old. Returning to my origins, to the infancy and youth common to all of us, I entered the door of my past and into the world of events that flow like a river and that take us into the future.

Returning to my studies of the first philosophers, the pre-Socratics, I understood that today, more than ever, we need to study, once again, the essential elements of the universe. This is not so much the physical-chemical composition, more the mythical-spiritual relation of man and the universe, and the potential for transforming man's spirit.

From this moment, transformation became a key word for me, which I would keep on the shelves of my heart with great devotion and respect: transformation, transmutation, metamorphosis. Through this concept, I could see how the different and contrasting trends of rational and mythical thinking, from our Greek childhood, would flow through the 'rosy fingered dawn' and 'wine-dark sea'.

What many of these philosophical trends had in common was that they were taught in gardens, in outdoor spaces enclosed by walls, where, under porticos, the students learned to listen. In the midst of these cloisters full of vegetation, the murmuring of the water from the fountain accompanied the dialogues and the moments of silence of Plato in the garden of Academos and Aristotle in the garden of Liceo. There was also Epicurus, who had a labyrinth planted at the entrance to his garden in order to obstruct those who were not determined to make the effort to reach its centre: the garden of the master, the garden of dialogue and of knowledge.

It was this discovery, and this evidence, and this way of being and feeling, that made me decide to transform, transmute and undergo the metamorphosis from young philosopher to ancient gardener. I say 'gardener' because this mythical word belongs to mankind and contains memories of our purest origins, so full of resonance and touching aspects both elemental and fragile. Not for nothing was a garden the first domain that the gods gave us, and in it we keep the memories and sacred images that will always take us back to this beginning.

Garden and gardener: these are words that belong to a source language and have been asleep, silenced by terror and the uncivil past century, but that today flourish and offer us comfort like the crystal-clear water that returns to our minds the essence and the need to forget so much barbarity. Garden and gardener, two words that have the power of transformation that help us recapture memories of childhood and lead us to a future where we can once again interpret the dream of life.

Because of all of this, I have changed. My desire to become a philosopher became a desire to become a gardener. This way of thinking is much more powerful than my fear of it; despite my resistance, it transforms me. I undergo a metamorphosis that one day will awaken me, just like the characters in *A Midsummer Night's Dream* – sometimes I am a satyr, at other times a foolish human, but always an astonished gardener.

Astonished gardener, who was one day reading Pythagoras

and understood the power of geometry. 'Everything is in the number', this enigmatic master would say. 'Those who are not familiar with geometry should not enter this academy', Plato would say to his students from the portico.

I recalled my geometry class at school and the tedious drawings that seemed incomprehensible to us but that we rendered automatically. I could not understand these mysterious sentences that continued to echo in my head. How was it possible that after I had studied geometry for all those years, it was not only uninteresting to me, but the fascinating power held within those geometries had not been revealed to me? Those geometric figures did not help me to comprehend something more, the something that Plato said was of paramount importance, an absolute necessity. It was then that I began to analyze the drawings that I had done at the gardening school and the designs for gardens that I had begun to undertake. I was truly discovering geometry in its most elemental and straightforward form: the geometry of the point, the line and the angle that makes up the grid form, which, in a totally unconscious manner, I was developing in my projects.

Then I discovered that my hand knew things that I took for granted, that my hand traced signs on the paper and arranged space with a method that I had not learnt but that I had probably inherited; it was a maternal language, ancient and forgotten, essential. It helped me to babble my first gardens.

It was the language and grammar of geometry that gave me the forgotten codes that enabled me to encounter space and to invoke it through the garden. I realized that I was in some way in contact with 'the spirit of the geometrician', a spirit that dwells in the Greek childhood of man, returning one to its enigmas and providing the geometry required to reveal them. I recalled a lecture about Vitruvius and Pliny the Younger that concerned the spirit of place and how its language was nothing other than geometric.

The grid became a fishing net, a net that you cast into space and that returns full of the most amazing treasures from the bottom of the sea: starfish, winkle, giant octopus, and semi-human forms that you restore to the sea feeling completely astonished.

The grid is a gift that helps you contemplate the stars, to measure the sky; it is the chessboard where the figures are moved, the infinite space where the gardener, the musician, the archae-ologist, the astronaut, express their interior worlds. Then the miracle is repeated. You only have to believe that you can throw the fishing net into space time and time again, a thousand times over, to collect that treasure from space.

From this grid, and using the master key of the golden section, the world of corresponding spatial relationships is opened. Correspondence between the setsquare, the triangle, the circle, the pentagon, the decagon: geometric figures that reveal the analogies between man and the universe. These analogies appear when we are faced with a project; they give us the key to understanding the dynamic symmetries, musical rhythms and cadences that nature hides. It is geometry that transforms sensations into art and translates concepts into science.

Pythagoras, Plato and the neo-Platonists, Piero della Francesca, Paccioli, Leonardo, Dürer, Alberti, Dante and Petrarch – some use the base of the pentagram and others the symbol of man as a microcosm; all of these figures use the scale of the golden section as a measurement for all things. Poets, philosophers, gardeners, scientists, musicians, chemo-perfumers and artists have all followed, at different stages of our history, the river of universal geometry.

This is our inheritance, a thread of clear water that slowly rises inside the cave while nearby a cool breeze rises at dawn. This is our inheritance, a great inheritance that we must treasure and protect, that we must pass on from generation to generation so that man can once again exceed himself and accomplish the sacred task of seeing, together with the realization that as well as

THE SPIRIT OF THE GEOMETRICIAN

hell and purgatory, paradise is also possible on this earth that we have been given.

In appreciation of your patience in having read these lines written by an apprentice gardener, I would like to finish with the first verses of the *Divine Comedy* of Dante, words that continue to inspire us all:

> Midway upon the journey of our life
> I found myself within a forest dark,
> For the straightforward pathway had been lost.
>
> Ah me! how hard a thing it is to say
> what was this forest savage, rough, and stern,
> which in the very thought renews the fear.
>
> So bitter is it, death is little more;
> but of the good to treat, which there I found,
> speak will I of the other things I saw there.
>
> I cannot well repeat how there I entered,
> so full was I of slumber at the moment
> in which I had abandoned the true way.

ZEN AND THE ART OF TEA GARDENING

Charles Chesshire

The so-called 'Zen' garden of raked gravel has become an enduring design cliché, founded on faulty historical references. This essay advances the idea that designs inspired by the traditional Japanese tea garden might have more resonance for contemporary Western gardens.

In trying to explain the unanticipated harmony between English and Japanese football fans during the World Cup in 2002, a journalist described the two archipelago nations as being like 'twins separated at birth'. Twins that took a long time to find each other, and are still perhaps a little bewildered by each other's culture, England and Japan do have much in common, not least their common obsession with gardens and tea. This essay explores the Japanese tea and gardens theme, looking to it as a possible new source of inspiration for Western gardeners who want to build bridges between urban life and nature, and between Eastern and Western cultures.

The English managed to maintain only a toehold in Japan, for a very brief period in the early 1600s, before the Tokugawa shogunate, tired of the squabbles between traders from various European nations, closed their country down to foreigners for more than 200 years. In the following two centuries, Chinese culture came to influence the development of the English landscape garden, but Japan would remain a mystery until she was forced open again by the Americans in 1865.

The period from 1865 to the 1930s saw designers and architects such as Charles Rennie Mackintosh in Britain and Frank

Lloyd Wright in the United States being influenced by the arts and architecture of Japan, but little in the way of Japanese garden art reached England. An 'authentic' Japanese tea garden was constructed in the 1920s in Tatton Park in Cheshire, but a visiting Japanese ambassador, although politely impressed, observed that nothing like it existed in Japan.

Most of the motifs of the Japanese garden developed in the golden age that lasted from 1500 to the late 1700s. By the early 1900s Japanese gardens had begun to decline, often lacking true meaning or becoming poor copies of themselves, full of clichés and empty devices. By the 1930s, artist Mirei Shigemori had recognized this and began a revitalization of the genre. While staying true to old motifs and traditional materials, he radically 'modernized' the Japanese garden by breathing new life into its spirit. Subsequent designers in Japan have taken this abstraction further by using modern materials such as cut rocks, plastics and metal, but most continue to refer back to the traditions of Japanese garden making.

The English garden, some might argue, was suffering the same kind of tiredness by the 1950s. The last time the English garden possessed any kind of formal or philosophical language was during the development of the landscape and Picturesque gardens of the eighteenth century, a language which, however, did not translate to later gardens in terms of either scale or ideology. The later 'cottage garden' style, based as it is more on horticulture than design, does not possess the kind of formal dynamism sought by contemporary designers. It has therefore been difficult to revitalize English garden design, and attempts at contemporary English gardens make scant reference to the country's traditions and past forms.

The model that has emerged – the contemporary garden, which fills our television screens and magazines – evolved instead from an attraction to the superficial aesthetics of abstraction and minimalism, coupled with ease of maintenance. With a good dose of reductionism, these so-called contemporary gardens are often regarded as relating to the Japanese garden tradition, or even described as 'Zen'. Utilizing clean-polished and high-quality materials such as marble, stainless steel and decking, they operate under the guise of austerity. But the slick functionalism behind many of these gardens actually expresses a sheer opulence that is really in stark opposition to the ascetic principles of Zen. Gunter Nitzchke, an architect, academic and yogi based in Kyoto, describes this quasi-epidemic reference to Zen as Zennism. All manner of things are described these days as 'so very Zen' and one cannot place a rock in gravel or sand without someone making a passing reference to Zen or Japan.

What these so-called Zen gardens of rocks and sand do refer to is actually a very specific type of garden called *kare-sansui* – literally meaning 'dry mountain water'. As Nitzchke points out, these owe as much to Shinto and Chinese landscape painting as they do to Zen. It might be more valid to view these dry gardens as the Japanese equivalent of the European Picturesque, as their inspiration too came from painting: the landscape paintings of twelfth-century China. The Ryoanji in Kyoto, laid out in 1499, is the most perfect, and well-known example of this type of garden: the principal ingredients are fifteen moss-fringed rocks, exquisitely spaced in perfect proportions and framed in a perfect rectangular sea of gravel.

This garden style would not come to the awareness of the West until nearly 400 years after it was first developed in Japan. The late nineteenth century was a time when esoteric and mystical spiritual paths, many inspired by the East, were being actively sought out. More recently, Zen spirituality and all its artistic offshoots, from gardening to martial arts, have appealed to the spiritual and artistic aspirations of many in the West.

Very few people actually practise Zen in the West but many have a vague understanding of what is meant by it. Quiet meditation is a luxury that most of us only wish we had more time for, but there is more to Zen: one of its great secrets can be found in its 'active' part. Zen is not simply about austerity and meditation but also about developing a serene outlook, a disciplined composure derived from a calm interior. The goal is a perfect steadiness of mind that is reflected in the way we act in the world. In those simple Japanese stone and gravel temple gardens, what we are seeing is the tranquil perfection that reflects the inner world of the priests and abbots who made and maintain them. The 'action' of raking the sand in the *kare-sansui*, for instance, is one of the spiritual practices of Zen priests.

In Japan the highly esteemed disciplines of painting, calligraphy, poetry and gardening have become imbued with the spirit of Zen, yet they all have their roots in China. It was Japanese Buddhist priests who introduced Zen and these relatively humble art forms from China and raised them to new levels of refinement. This aptitude for digesting the culture of their larger continental neighbours to make their own pearls is another trait shared with England.

It is easy to see why *kare-sansui* gardens have captured imaginations in the West and how its convenience and simplicity could act as an inspiration for the modern garden, especially a city garden. But there is another kind of Japanese garden that has been largely unexplored and is perhaps even better suited to being translated to the West. The Japanese tea garden, the *roji* or *cha-niwa*, has also evolved with a Zen influence, and the principles behind it are admirably suited for translation into a modern Western context. It even has a strong horticultural aspect, less apparent in the *kare-sansui*, which might give it additional appeal to those who work in the English tradition of plantsmanship.

The tea garden was originally simply a path called the *roji*. *Roji* literally can be translated as 'dewy path', a name that reflects its derivation. Many Chinese painters of the twelfth century were members of the literati: poets, artists and philosophers who, uninterested in court life under the occupying Mongols, retired to the mountains to write poetry and to paint pictures. The subject for their paintings was the world they had chosen to make their own, such as their bamboo huts and caves in the mountains. While Japanese Zen priests had found in these paintings a graphic inspiration for the *kare-sansui* gardens, the lifestyle, bamboo huts and rituals of the hermit artists would become the main source of inspiration for the tea ceremony, tea house and the tea garden. On their journeys to reach these hermitages the priests would have had to scramble along paths damp with dew that crossed over mountain streams through the misty wilderness, treading a dewy path.

In the sixteenth and seventeenth centuries, enlightened members of merchant and samurai classes chose to bring the world of the dewy path into their city gardens. The bamboo huts and rustic hermitages evolved into sophisticated tea houses and gardens that their owners would refer to as their 'mountain place in the city', where they could enjoy the realm of the tranquil while still immersed in the worldliness of city life. The paths that they had beaten in the wild became the main motif for the *roji*. These new hermitages within the city came to be regarded as superior to the real thing and, of course, a great deal more comfortable. The *roji*, often only a few metres in extent, would save the epic struggle of scrambling through forests and over mountain streams.

The tea path, initially a series of stepping stones leading to the tea house itself, developed into something far more elaborate, passing through a series of gates and small waiting pavilions. Pure mountain water would lay fresh, cool and still in special basins to purify minds and bodies, while stone lanterns lit the way, as the tea ceremony was often conducted in the evening. In the tea house, merchants, samurai and even the shogun could bridge their social divide over an elaborate tea ceremony, frequently accompanied by a light meal. The tea ceremony provided a secular vehicle for social, spiritual and aesthetic exchanges, with Zen present in the sense of the self-awareness that derives from the ritual of walking the path and the practice of the ceremony itself. Under the guidance of celebrated tea masters between about 1500 and the 1650s, tea houses and tea gardens became increasingly sophisticated city constructs, refined by poets, rich merchants and aspiring literati.

One of the more eccentric and gifted Japanese tea masters was Oribe (1544–1615), who introduced personal taste and playfulness to the tea path. Oribe took the *roji*, the path, and made it into a garden, *cha-niwa*. He mixed natural and dressed stone, placed ocean pebbles in the outer *roji* and spread pine needles under the wilder shrubs of the inner *roji*. He no longer imitated nature in its outer form, but brought to it an individualism that had largely been lost since the formalizing of the codes of tea. In his garden, the play of the shadows of bamboo, the subtlety of moonlight and an atmosphere of romantic rusticity could be enjoyed without having to endure the danger and filth of country life. Oribe was a rebellious samurai whose excesses eventually incurred the wrath of the shogun. He committed suicide in 1615. His master was the great Rikyu, the patron saint of tea, who twenty-five years earlier had also incurred the displeasure of his superiors, and was forced to disembowel himself in his own rustic tea house.

The design of the tea house is a matter of taste. One ostentatious shogun had a gilded portable tea house built to entertain the emperor, yet in one of its earliest incarnations it was merely a miscanthus grass-covered hovel. In some instances, the tea house may become a simple tea room integrated with the main house, but the journey to it is always via the *roji*.

In Kyoto I was once shown a modern *roji* by an aging Danish hippy who was teaching the tea ceremony from his home there.

His tea path was all of five or six metres long, but at each step we stopped to note a view, a hidden Hindu statue or to admire a fern collected from the slopes of sacred Mount Heie, or an aza-lea given to him by a neighbour. The garden tour took half an hour before stopping off for a while at the tea house itself. The Dane's unique interpretation of the *roji* was proof, for me, that the theme was still relevant.

The term *roji* was used metaphorically by the great tea master Rikyu to signify that the mind was purified and had taken leave of worldly toil and defilement, but in the tangible world *roji* expresses its purity in the form of trees and rocks. Zen and the art of tea merge to represent more than the physical presence of the garden – in Zen, the *roji* becomes open space, a metaphor for the space occupying the realm beyond human life. In Western terms this might be seen as a gateway to paradise or the equiva-lent of the lost Garden of Eden.

Along the *roji* stand various buildings, beginning with a simple sheltered seat, a place to wait quietly to be called for tea by the host. After being summoned for tea, one usually passes through the *naka-kuguri*, or 'middle crawl-through gate'. This gate acts as a reflective signpost, shifting our attention away from the world that we are leaving behind and towards an awareness of the higher realm that we are approaching. The gate itself may be an elaborate affair, or simply indicated by a post designed to awaken that awareness.

After passing under or through the 'middle crawl-through gate', we enter the inner *roji*, the garden that approaches the tea house. Evoking a path deep in the wilderness, this crucial space is often represented in garden terms by mountain shrubs and flowers. To me this treatment of the wilderness, as a rare jewel to be approached with reverence, is where the true genius of the tea garden lies.

Simmering away under the high-energy fabric of our society there is undeniably a growing yearning for a more harmonious relationship with the world. The current trend for wild gardens, meadows and naturalized woodland plantings all reflect the longing for a lost wilderness and our hopes for a restoration of lost ecologies. For the modern-day literati, a tea house and the dewy path leading to it can be a potent means of manifesting and 'inhabiting' that wilderness, a way of finding a sense of equanimity. In the tea garden, the wilderness can be brought to the centre of the garden, while our 'mountain place in the city' can express a yearning to live in the wilderness, especially as the city dweller often finds the real thing too much to bear.

Both the English and the Japanese have a genius for appropriating ideas, art and culture, and assimilating them in such a unique way that their new arts and culture are seen as their own. For centuries these 'twins' have been crushing the grist of their 'older' neighbours in order to create their own genius. Now, at a time when the Japanese garden is appropriating ideas from the English style of gardening, I believe that the new English garden could crush some of that Zen sand, and instead of creating thoughtless imitations, digest it to form new pearls of their own.

Creating a modern *roji* is not as challenging as it may first appear. We already use many of the elements of the tea garden, such as stepping-stones, garden lights and water basins. Our shed or summer-house could easily be adapted for spiritual, social and artistic discourse, whilst all manner of variations on the tea house can be built without too much difficulty. Our love of naturalistic plantings could find a great outlet in echoing the native Japanese wilderness. Our own wilderness could be manifested as a meadow or a woodland walk.

But of course there is one more twist in the tealeaf. Once we have contemplated the world of the great tea masters, their collected calm, their lightly trod paths, perhaps we need not rip up the lawn or the roses and thatch our gazebos, but simply view our garden as a journey with a sense of truth and equanimity.

Zen is more about a state of mind: perhaps all we really need to do is to imbue our garden with the spirit of Zen and tea, without changing a thing.

THE POWER IS IN HARMONY

Nori Pope and Sandra Pope

In this essay, the co-creators of the famous colour garden at Hadspen in Somerset describes how their planting methods are underpinned by ideas derived from music.

The garden, as with all arts, needs a language of words and images in order to develop co-ordinated thinking. With few exceptions we have been willing to use the language of horticulture, which can produce fantastically accurate catalogues of plants, but which advances no particular reasons for having them and certainly no process for developing aesthetic progress. The world of music hands us a sophisticated language of tone, colour and image in which to think. Grasp it!

Harmony – harmonic: 'a combination or arrangement of parts to form a consistent and orderly whole, agreement, congruity; agreeable effect.'

Waves of energy equally divisible are in a harmonic state. It is harmony that gives strength to our gardens, to our lives, to the spheres or static state of the cosmos described by Newton and taken up by Holst in 'The Planets'. Without harmony there is no power in contrast, merely aberration and chaos. In all aesthetic pursuits, whether gardening, painting, music or physics, it is seeking patterns in the seemingly random world around us that gives it meaning and pleasure.

Chaos is where there is one of every kind; it is the muddle of contrasting unrelated colours – a visual car crash of colour, an explosion of texture, a sampling of unrelated architectural styles. Simplicity is the other side of this spinning coin.

In an alpine meadow the plants are spaced with the rigid discipline of necessity. It is this ecological balance – with a limited range of plants, texture and colour – that gives such places a universal appeal. When we walk into a Frank Lloyd Wright house and the paths, the steps, the stairs are made from the same material, if they change texture it is with a sense of purpose, of necessity. A forest of beech, the pillars of the Parthenon, a field of sunflowers or a cityscape of skyscrapers draws us in. This gives us a sense of rightness, of pleasure. It is the logic of it that always works. This doesn't mean that plainness is the only path to a concordant whole, but it is a good place to begin.

To use colour, with control of the anticipated result, is the goal of gardeners who have gone past the point where merely growing the plant is enough. We know that yellow is in harmony with green, which is, of course, a mixture of blue and yellow and so contains the flavour of each. To develop a colour-themed garden is much like playing or singing a tune. The piece has a key, a rhythm and a melody. In the garden the same musical patterns emerge – the key could be yellow, taken up by both the flowers and foliage. The rhythm could be a repetition of a single shape, such as a daisy, carried from spring to autumn, beginning with varieties of doronicum, *Anemone lipsiensis*, *Anthemis tinctoria*, then varieties of tanacetum, and then finally to heleniums. A repetition of a plant grouping, for instance lupin 'Chandelier' growing through rose 'Golden Wings' and tangled through with the *Potentilla recta* 'Pallida', keep the melody moving along.

Our eyes are drawn to like colours, like objects and like patterns. When we look at a garden our eye will seek out a colour, perhaps a red flower, and then search for other red flowers throughout the garden. In the same way, if we see a particular shape – a verbascum flower spike, perhaps – we look for any other similar shape and connect them in our mind's eye. It is these connections that give the garden continuity and a sense of purposeful progression.

Having created a theme for your garden, it is time to decide what quality you want to experience when walking through it or sitting in it. Is it to be a pale pastel event, like faded flowery fabric, comfortable and undemanding? Or is it to be a dramatic build up of colour from yellow through oranges to a saturated red, as we have in our garden at Hadspen House? With pastels, for example, it is simply white mixed in with a colour that makes it into a pastel (for example, white with red makes pink). White is also the cohesive factor that holds the picture together. The reflective qualities of pastel colours give them an added lightness that whole-tone colours do not provide. Pure white, on the other hand, reflects the maximum amount of light back to us and so always stands out as brightest, overwhelming all its neighbours.

To take the hot border at Hadspen as an example of a theme, the harmony of the colour changes holds the picture together so that we can exploit the full theatrical impact of these scintillating shades. Dark purple-red foliage forms the backdrop, with *Phormium tenax* 'Purpureum Group' and *Prunus x cistena*, which creates a planting that is effective all winter. On the high brick wall behind, the purple-leaved grape, *Vitis vinifera* 'Purpurea', tangles with the vivid red of the single rose 'Altissimo'. During the summer they are underplanted with that incredible dahlia 'Bishop of Llandaff', whose red-black foliage and simple scarlet flowers with mandarin orange stamens is almost a whole planting scheme in itself. Self-seeding *Atriplex hortensis* var. rubra spreads throughout, strengthening the continuity of the undertone. In the foreground of this border, *Dianthus barbatus* 'Nigrescens', the dark-leaved Japanese sweet William with fragrant velvet flowers, are a perfect foil for the tulips 'Queen of the Night', 'Black Parrot' and 'Red Shine', with the dianthus foliage covering up the dying leaves of the tulips as spring turns to summer. The glowing red stems of ruby chard are too good to leave to the vegetable garden alone and find a place in any red planting. With the late summer sun backlighting *Crocosmia*

'Lucifer' and *Helenium* 'Moerheim Beauty', the flames are really licking the pyre.

Art is about intention and we feel the need to use the well-developed language of music to investigate and explore these intentions. For example, to say that a garden has coloratura elaborations is much more poetic and meaningful than explaining that the garden has a lot of flowery plants and attention to the details of colour organization.

Intention requires clarity of thought and purpose: a meandering path wiggling towards its goal of a door shows only the wishy-washy indecision of a television makeover, while pastiche post-modern architecture – with its mixture of architectural styles, every window a different shape and size, the cladding like a sales display from a DIY store – makes us want to reach for the wrecking ball. The reason we adore Georgian buildings and want to preserve them is because of their simplicity, their clarity of intent. The mountain meadow, however perfect, is not a garden – spilled paint might be interesting but it is not a Jackson Pollock. It is the cohesion and purpose of the event that gives a huge nests of sticks by Andy Goldsworthy the emotional hook and takes us to a different plane of looking, a new connection with Kierkegaard's idea about the fallen branch in the forest, and whether it has been heard or not as it falls.

As we gardeners are thinking about the planting of our garden, the pitfall many of us fall into is the collection. The desire to acquire every new or rare plant, or every piece of hardware, is good fun, of course, but it is not a route to a good garden. A field of ox-eye daisies and buttercups is the most perfect example of harmony, with the airy yellow buttercup flowers picking up the yellow of the daisy's eye. And what is more, it suddenly looks very fashionable, in a minimalist sort of way.

PSYCHOTOPIA

Tim Richardson

The author has formulated an updated version of Alexander Pope's idea of the genius of the place and its relation to gardens, in the light of the philosophies of phenomenology and existentialism.

Most thoughtful gardeners and garden designers consider a sense of place to be one of the defining aspects of the medium in which they work. Indeed, in many cases, this prevailing atmosphere or spirit is believed to be the most important and enriching variable of all. Although buildings and art objects are themselves apparently able to produce such tangible atmospheres or physical fields, it seems these cannot match the scale and intensity that is potentially offered by landscapes and gardens. If one wants to make a case for the unique strength of this art form, it is necessary to describe and define what it is that the medium can offer. It seems to me that an understanding of the spirit of place is key to this endeavour.

So what is this spirit of place, precisely? At the very least, it is clear that the meaning and one's experience of a place tends to be wrapped up in its invisible as well as its visible qualities. However, any empirical description of this spirit of place usually falls short; what gardens provide us with in terms of atmosphere cannot be easily anatomised. We have Alexander Pope's famous injunction, 'consult the genius of the place in all', and the various ancient traditions of animism. There are also the modern schools of humanistic, behavioural, aesthetic and psycho geography, as well as envirinmental psychology, and also the rich body of work on place theory that has arisen from that in the past thirty years or so. But these approaches tend either to reject unequivocally or take for granted as self-evident, the presence in nature of a spirit of place that exists externally of our own consciousness; they do not attempt to anatomise what that spirit actually is.[1]

The word place itself – so serviceable, in many ways, but used for meanings that range from the topographically banal to the philosophically profound – also seems inadequate in this context. In usage it is interchangeable with 'location', 'site', 'area', 'region' and even 'space', when each should really have quite separate definitions. The potentially useful 'milieu' also emerges as too vague. In recent years, the word place has been appropriated by geographers and others as a way of describing space that is freighted with meaning or character, but this appropriation effectively jargonizes the word, since it does not replace or transcend the word's other usages except in academic contexts. Which is why I offer up a new, more specific term – psychotopia – as a shorthand for a way of describing places as they are actually experienced in life, not how they are 'objectively' assessed, described later, or assimilated into existing theories. One could argue that we have enough words already, but my intention here is to increase, not decrease, our clarity of thought on this matter.

Psychotopia is place understood not just in terms of location, but also in terms of meaning – its history, use, ecology, appearance, status, reputation, the people who interact with the place, its potential future. It refers to the actual life of the place as it is experienced by those who visit it, and therefore also encapsulates the psychic impact and assimilation of human consciousnesses. It does not only describe the atmosphere of a place as apprehended by the human mind – the landscape is not passive in that sense – psychotopia addresses the dynamic manner in which the atmosphere of places works on us and, more controversially, how, in turn, our minds and experiences act on and influence places. Psychotopia is place seen anew, supercharged with meaning and life.

The word is an amalgam of 'psyche' and 'topos'. Topos refers to place, of course, but psyche, meaning mind or animating spirit, has a dual application here. It refers to the spirit of the place itself – its 'mind', which exists independently of us and can in a sense speak to us. It also refers to our own psyches, in that I would argue that we become co-creators of places as soon as we experience them, and inevitably influence the prevailing sense of place through our own interaction. (The idea for psychotopia in fact emerged from the realization that garden and landscape designers are, in a way, the psychoanalysts of places, which itself stemmed from Gaston Bachelard's coinage of 'topo-analysis'.[2]) Thus, the mental traffic travels both ways in a symbiotic process of mutual accretion: humans influence places; places influence humans. A psychotopia is a place where human psyche connects and combines with place psyche. This is not to suggest that a place might have a brain, free will or a personality in a quasi-human sense; but on the other hand, it is not to deny that a place can actively work on us, and that it can be possessed of a kind of memory, which can be expressed.

To make the case for psychotopia, three questions need to be addressed. First, do places have innate atmospheres? Second, do the mental interactions of human beings permanently affect places? Third, is place an index of our significance within the cosmos? I believe the answer in all three cases is in the affirmative. Let me say at the outset that I will be unable to produce empirical proof for any of these answers; they are not self-evident matters of fact. (Since we live in a scientific age, 'rational' readers might like to move on to the next essay at this point.) There is, however, a sound philosophical, emotional and intuitive basis for this attitude, which I will outline before proceeding to the questions.

THE PHILOSOPHICAL BACKGROUND OF PSYCHOTOPIA

The attitude to place and the aesthetics of landscape described in this essay represents a form of phenomenology, which emerged as one of the major strands of philosophical thinking in the twentieth century. I should state at the outset that psychotopia is not predicated on faith. It is not spiritual. It is not romantic. It is not irrational.

Phenomenology is a theory of knowledge that is descriptive rather than empiricist, and as such represents a departure from the prevailing, avowedly commonsensical tradition of philosophy that has flourished in Britain since the eighteenth century. The first proponent of phenomenology as a distinct philosophical stance was Edmund Husserl (1859–1938), although the most influential thinker of this loose movement (it could not be called a school, since there are quite different emphases in the work of each philosopher, and they change over time) was probably Martin Heidegger (1889–1976). Jean-Paul Sartre's existentialism was another version of phenomenology (indeed, the two philosophies have become synonymous for some commentators) and more recently Jacques Derrida's methodology is described (at least by Derrida himself) as phenomenological in its basis.

The essence of phenomenology is Husserl's idea of returning things to themselves, of seeing the world (or 'lifeworld', in phenomenological jargon – meaning life as it is actually lived) without preconceptions, theories or hypotheses and instead with a sense of wonderment and intuitive clarity. Husserl suggested that we try to 'bracket' out of the world the object of experience, so that even our belief in its reality is suspended. By doing this, we might return to the essential facts or fundamental structures of experience. This aim is palpably impossible, but for the phenomenological thinker it is the method, the experience, that is important, not its 'success'.

Heidegger wrote of 'the power of letting things manifest themselves' and of the importance of 'Being' as the key to the existence of all things and the source of all our understanding. Any overarching theoretical apparatus is therefore instinctively mistrusted and our observations of the flow of experience are ideally unfettered by preconceived ideas. The centrality of the body to mind and intelligence ('the embodied mind'), and the relationship of the human body with the world, quickly emerged as of crucial importance in phenomenological thought, and this was explored particularly deeply in the work of both Heidegger and Maurice Merleau-Ponty. A fundamental realization is that space (in the geometrical, Euclidean sense, or in the physical, Newtonian sense) is not the organizing principle of place; it is the indivisible mind and body that are. Place emerges as describable neither in physical nor psychological terms alone, or even combined. As Heidegger put it: 'When we speak of man and space, it sounds as though man stood on one side, space on the other. Yet space is not something that faces man. It is neither an external object nor an inner experience.'

So what has phenomenology got to do with landscapes and gardens? Phenomenological thinkers who have treated of aesthetics (chiefly Heidegger, Merleau-Ponty and Roman Ingarden) have tended to concentrate on the established arts: literature, painting, dance, theatre, sculpture, and, to some extent, architecture and music. This is not so much a conscious repudiation of the aesthetic potential of landscapes and gardens, more a reflection of their historically lowly position in the hierarchy of the arts, which is akin to that of Norway in the Eurovision Song Contest. In fact it seems to me that garden- and landscape-making, in all its changefulness, uncertainty and intensity of essence, is the phenomenological art form par excellence, because it reflects the way garden designers and garden visitors instinctively think. It is also an open door into the metaphysical world of sense of place.

When we recall a garden or landscape that we have visited in the past, what we conjure up is not a forensically formulated table of all the variables that worked upon us at the time (a 'landscape assessment'), but a single overall feeling of the essence of the place. It comes to us in a flash. This may be difficult – impossible, in fact – to describe in words, but that sense of place is real and important; it is just that in contemporary discourse it has been routinely downgraded or ignored in favour of other 'information'. It is embarrassing or gauche to talk about it or write about it. I would argue, however, that it is desirable that we engage with these deep personal feelings of place and attempt to give them voice as best we can, and in the best phenomenological spirit. The way I have tried to do this in my job as a gardens writer is by making sure that I use up some of my precious wordlength in describing the atmospheres of places as they seem to me, related to the visible and invisible characteristics of the garden – that is, in addition to more conventional information and observation. It is actually not a controversial thing to do (in the other arts, there is some correlation with a recent movement of 'descriptive aesthetics'[3]), particularly when one is discussing, say, early eighteenth-century landscapes, where associative meaning is so important.

The fact is, we all experience gardens in this way; it is the explication that is often unfinished. As Heidegger put it: 'The essence of art can no more be arrived at by a derivation from higher concepts than by a collection of characteristics of actual art works.'[4] Without the transformative participation of the observer, the aesthetic moment is incomplete. In addition, in the phenomenological attitude there is no doubt that experiences, including those that are 'abstract', have an actual basis in fact, and this holds for the truths of art, too. Thus, for Heidegger, beauty is not merely an optical effect but an innate presence in the world, and it can form a part of the essential Being of any object: 'The origin of the work of art is not in some inner vision

within the artist or within the spectator but in the truth of Being
that is already out there.' In a landscape or garden, that truth of
Being can be expressed as the sense of place.

One valuable ally in the struggle for acceptance of a non-
empiricist worldview is the twentieth-century philosopher-
mathematician Alfred North Whitehead (1861–1947), who
found fame early on as co-author with Bertrand Russell of
Principia Mathematica (1910) and later devised a unique and complex idea for a 'speculative philosophy' or metaphysics that is
based on the premise that the universe is in a state of constant
flux, that there is no reality without process. In his magnum
opus, *Process and Reality* (1929), and from his position as a theoretical scientist (Cambridge, Harvard, London), Whitehead bril-
liantly attacked as itself irrational the positivistic rejection of
metaphysics: the idea that general principles about the nature of
things are unattainable unless backed up by empirical research.
He argued instead: 'If science is not to degenerate into a medley
of ad hoc hypotheses, it must become philosophical and must
enter upon a thorough criticism of its own foundations.'
Whitehead suggested that since Einstein, scientific ideas had
become grounded in theory rather than phenomena that are
observable by ordinary people. The phenomenologists echoed
this idea with their criticism of an autonomous science, which
simplifies abstractions by creating theoretical constructs that
stand up by themselves but have no relation to life experience.

Merleau-Ponty suggested: 'It is the mission of the twentieth
century to elucidate the irrational'.[5] Whitehead argued that the
best way of achieving this is to base the methodology of the natural sciences in actual, lived experience, rather than in the habit-
ual modes of thought of empiricism. For Whitehead, this choice
has serious practical repercussions for humanity: 'Suppose a hundred thousand years ago our ancestors had been wise positivists.
They sought for no reasons. What they had observed was sheer
matter of fact. It was the development of no necessity. They

would have searched for no reasons underlying facts immediately observed. Civilisation would never have developed.'[6] The non-empirical approach might lead to a certain indistinctness and imprecision, but such ambiguity is seen not as a defect but as a potential strength for science, if it had the courage to grasp it. Indeed, for Whitehead, the clarity and 'watertight' nature of a theory is usually evidence of its inherent weakness rather than its strength.[7]

The phenomenological or Whiteheadian basis for psychotopia is not advanced as some kind of belief system that one might subscribe to. In certain crucial respects – in the dimensions of personal relationships and of politics, notably (Heidegger was a member of the Nazi party from 1933 to 1945; Sartre was an apologist for Stalin) – phenomenology is wholly inadequate. In any context, it is a vivid descriptive methodology rather than a coldly calculated unified theory. With reference to gardens and landscapes (and the allied topic of the concept of home), it appears that the phenomenological perspective is ripe for study, and might provide us with insights that conventional rational explication cannot. There are lots of ideas in the ensuing pages. Taken together, or even in quite small sections, they do not form coherent, supportable arguments, but that, in the context of a phenomenological perspective, is part of the point. Whether or not they are useful is another matter.

SPIRIT OF PLACE AS AN INDEPENDENT ENTITY

So to the first question: do places have innate atmospheres? It is generally accepted that landscapes and gardens are imbued with meanings that are derived from how and why we know them, and who we are. The perceived properties of all objects depend on the personality and culture of the viewer; therefore, as we perceive a place visually, we instantaneously interpret its meanings. Each person sees each place in a different way – in this sense, we see gardens not as they are, but as we are. Edward Relph has summarized this attitude to place:

> The individuality of places and landscapes differs in one fundamental aspect from that of people. It is accorded rather than self-created. A landscape is always an aggregation of objects and organisms arranged in a singular pattern which is the product of the interaction of physical, ecological, historical, economic and random processes. There is no single inner force directing and co-ordinating all of these. Yet it seems as though there is an individuality which lies behind the forms and appearances and maintains a coherent identity. We know that the spirit of a place can persist through countless changes in detail and structure. For instance, in a village which has existed for centuries it is quite possible that every building will have been reconstructed at least once, and they will all have been repeatedly changed in the course of maintenance and repair. There may also have been drastic changes to the fabric of the village – new churches, roads and housing estates being added to the existing ones. However, there can be little question that this is the same essential place that it has always been.[8]

Relph goes on to ascribe the longevity of the spirit of place to traditional building techniques, and the care and responsibility of locals. Now, this sounds 'rational' enough, but perhaps it is not quite enough. It is not psychotopia. From a phenomenological standpoint, one cannot categorize and mentally file away the powerfully felt sense of place so easily. Just because every individual experiences each place in their own unique way, it does not necessarily follow that places are bereft of innate qualities. After all, it is widely accepted, in terms of everyday experience, that places seem to exude their own atmospheres, irrespective of our predispositions. As the architectural theorist (and Heideggerian) Christian Norberg-Schulz argues: 'The existential dimension is not "determined" by the socio-economical conditions, although they may facilitate or impede the (self-) realisation of certain existential structures. The socio-economical conditions are like a picture frame; they offer a certain "space" for life to take place, but do not determine its existential meanings. The existential meanings have deeper roots.'[9]

Some natural settings seem to possess a character largely derived from the topography and the way the plants and trees are grouped, and perhaps it is this alone which produces a sense of the spirit of a place, the consistent space flavour that emanates from the place and which is then absorbed and transmuted by all the different people who experience it. Man seems instinctively to ascribe spiritual values to natural places. In Ancient Greece, places with pronounced natural qualities were associated with particular deities: for example, places with a fertile atmosphere were dedicated to Demeter and Hera, places where man works for and against nature were associated with Apollo, and mountains with a 360-degree view were dedicated to Zeus.[10] But perhaps it is more useful to examine the question from the standpoint of aesthetics rather than spirituality, which is precisely what the contemporary phenomenological aesthetician Arnold Berleant has done in studies such as *The Aesthetics of Environment* (2005). 'The human environment', he writes, 'has sensory richness, directness and immediacy, together with cultural patterns and meanings that perception carries, and these give environment its thick texture. Environment, then, is a complex idea, the more so when we consider it aesthetically.'[11]

Gardens and landscapes are complex places, whether we like it or not. It is impossible to conceive of them simply as agglomerations of surface detail. A famous gardener once wrote, of a visit to Charles Jencks's cosmological landscape in Scotland, that he did not care for the meanings of gardens as long as they are nice places to be. This might sound like a refreshingly bracing stripping-away of theory and dogma to get to the basic essentials, but the deliberate blocking-out of the emergent meanings of places is not just an act of aesthetic sabotage but also a psychological impossibility, incompatible with philosophical and emotional honesty. It is a conceit – an artificial, self-conscious and highly stylized construct – but one that proves irresistible to the anti-intellectual strain in British culture, particularly when it comes to gardens.

The idea that mental constructs might appear in nature was developed by Whitehead: 'Scientific reasoning is completely dominated by the presupposition that mental functionings are not properly part of Nature...This sharp division between mentality and Nature has no ground in our fundamental observation . . .We should conceive mental operations as among the factors which make up the constitution of Nature.'[12] Whitehead saw no fundamental division between the human body and the surrounding universe, and suggested that we are too dependent on visual sense impressions for our understanding of the world. Poetry and literature can certainly give us more accurate 'information' about a place than photographs or other pseudo-objective data; I know this not just intuitively, but from practice as a writer and historian. A supporting point is made for different ends by Lisa Heschong in *Thermal Delight in Architecture* (1979): 'Since each sense contributes a slightly different perception of the world, the more senses involved in a particular experience, the fuller, the rounder, the experience becomes. If sight allows for a three-dimensional world, then each other sense contributes at least one, if not more, additional dimensions. The most vivid, powerful experiences are those involving all of the senses at once.' The vivid, multi-sensory experience that Heschong selects as her example is that of the Islamic garden (although a garden from any other culture would also have sufficed).

The closest description of the process of landscape perception in mainstream phenomenology comes in Merleau-Ponty's

Phenomenology of Perception (1962). The Parisian street scene is a refreshingly glamorous philosophical metaphor:

> In the natural attitude, I do not have perceptions, I do not posit this object as beside that one, along with their objective relationships, I have a flow of experiences which imply and explain each other both simultaneously and successively. Paris for me is not an object of many facets, a collection of perceptions, nor is it the law governing all these perceptions. Just as a person gives evidence of the same emotional essence in his gestures with his hands, in his way of walking and in the sound of his voice, each express perception occurring in my journey through Paris – the cafes, people's faces, poplars along the quays, the bends of the Seine – stands out against the city's whole being, and merely confirms that there is a certain style or a certain significance which Paris possesses. And when I arrived there for the first time, the first roads that I saw as I left the station were, like the first words spoken by a stranger, simply manifestations of a still ambiguous essence, but one already unlike any other. Just as we do not see the eyes of a familiar face, but simply its look and its expression, so we perceive hardly any object. There is present a latent significance, diffused throughout the landscape or the city, which we find in something specific and self-evident, which we feel no need to define.[13]

That passing reference to landscape in the last sentence is, perhaps, all the encouragement we need. And of course – contrary to Merleau-Ponty's assertion – when a place (a landscape or garden) is perceived as an aesthetic object, we do in fact feel the urge to define its characteristics and meaning.

The humanistic values that we find in places are again reflected in the aesthetic theories of the Polish phenomenologist Roman Ingarden (1893–1970) (who unfortunately never wrote about gardens, despite his surname): 'A work of art has an enduring identity which transcends the multiplicity of mental acts and physical reproductions, but it is not timeless, it has a birth day, it changes in the course of history, and it can eventually die.'[14] Here the phenomenological aesthetic can be seen to be peculiarly suited to landscapes and gardens. A later phenomenological writer on aesthetics, Mikel Dufrenne, used the example of a public park in winter to illustrate the enduring nature, through change and decay, of the essence of a work of art: 'When I go for a walk in the park, it is still an idea that I perceive, but one that is perceptible to the eye and delivers a certain expression: nobility and measure here, abandon and caprice there, intimacy and tenderness elsewhere. The aesthetic object is always a language.'[15] In practice, our aesthetic appreciation of gardens and landscapes includes value judgements based on our appraisal of the effects of the garden and also our understanding of its essence. Christian Norberg-Schultz has commented on the enduring nature of the power of great works of art: 'The value of great works of art consists in their allowing for different interpretations without losing their identity. The different "interpretations" offered by a "chaotic form", on the contrary, are only arbitrary projections of the self, which burst like soap-bubbles.'[16] In this reading, great works of art are underpinned by a kind of strong essential order, while 'chaotic form' inspires various, weak and diffuse sentiments. So although every place is a psychotopia, some psychotopias are richer than others. Gardens and landscapes are among the richest of all because it is in them that we formalize our relationship with the cosmos.

Arnold Berleant notes the importance in a garden or landscape experience of physical engagement with the environment, our bodily experience, and the unusually insistent presence (for a work of art) of complex sensory qualities. But that is not quite the whole story: 'There is, moreover, an invisible dimension to environments, just as in the more visual arts. But here again it has a strength and vividness for the body that may be more compelling than on other aesthetic occasions.' We sense psychotopia in a palpably physical manner. Yet regardless of multi-sensory delights, places are defined for us by emotion and imagination rather than physical, sensory or spatial criteria. Berleant concludes: 'Environmental experience is, then, aesthetically rich. It infuses the most exceptional occasions with deep resonances of association and meaning. And it provides an inexhaustible opportunity for enlarging our perception, for discovering ourselves in discovering our world.'[17] That helps explain the strange and powerful pull or hold that places exert on us.

We tend to think of and refer to places as expressive of human emotion; they seem to have moods; they seem to be able to speak to us. Equally, we describe our emotions in turns of place. So when people talk of drug addiction or acute depression they say things like, 'I was in a very dark place at that period in my life' (at least they do on daytime television). There is also the question of where a place might end and begin. Places are not tidily stacked against each other. They are fluid, like all emotional experience. On one level a place exists as abstract thought, and on another level it exists as direct experience. Considered as a whole experience, scale emerges as far less important than we might have thought: we can have a relationship with a broom cupboard as a place, or a relationship with the continent of Africa as a place; the defining criterion of that relationship will not be physical size but emotional attachment. This is how landscape can inspire painters. Merleau-Ponty returned repeatedly to the subject of Cézanne, noting the crucial distinction that he did not paint landscapes – he painted the landscapes of Provence. In other words, the visual component was not necessarily the painter's paramount concern in terms of his inspiration: 'What motivates the painter's movement can never be simply perspective or geometry or the laws governing colour, or, for that matter, particular knowledge. Motivating all the movements from which a picture gradually emerges, there can be only one thing: the landscape in its totality and its absolute fullness, precisely what Cézanne called a "motif".[18] This is also how garden and landscape designers operate. In such a relationship, one has a palpable sense that the place is playing a role, rather than passively reflecting our self-generated ideas. If that is the case, it is a dialogue. Place becomes psychotopia.

Lest one thinks such an approach is inherently illogical, we could turn to Henry H. Price, Wykeham Professor of Logic at Oxford in the 1960s and 1970s. He suggested that: 'There is nothing self-contradictory or logically absurd in the hypothesis that memories, desires and images can exist in the absence of a physical brain.' In applying this hypothesis to a landscape or garden, we might decide that somehow the impressions or memories of its previous incarnations, and the effects of visitors or owners, can somehow become woven into the fabric of the place and transmit themselves to later visitors.

WE ARE CO-CREATORS

As garden visitors or owners, I would argue we are not just passive observers. We are co-creators, and every time we experience a garden we remake it for ourselves and others, physically and mentally.[19] In this most mutable of art forms, the physical appearance of the place and its ecological diversity might actually be less important to the sense of place than the cumulative meanings accorded it by previous visitors. Gardens and landscapes are not unique in that visitors participate in the creation work of art – in painting, Ernst Gombrich first pointed out our role as the co-creators in terms of optical effects[20] – but our interactions are perhaps more profound and dynamic. By some unquantifiable but describable process, the meanings accorded to a place by successive visitors, and the nature of their interaction with it, become absorbed: every time we visit a landscape we contribute something to its richness. The ghostly impressions of our interaction may be faint or imperceptible but they are there nevertheless. One has a forceful sense of the human contribution when coming across, for example, wheelbarrows, scaffolding, tools and piles of earth in a landscape garden. The workers or gardeners are gone, but the evidence of them lends the scene a sense of pathos, of curiosity, of anticipation or even annoyance. They have unknowingly altered the place by leaving traces of their presence.

People can have different kinds of relationships with gardens: as part of a community, on an individual level (as an owner, visitor or worker) and in terms of a legacy after death. I will describe each of these, then briefly speculate as to the actual processes involved with co-creation.

The Chinese-American aesthetic geographer Yi-Fu Tuan believes space becomes place as it becomes better known and is endowed with value, and psychological and symbolic meaning: the garden is made into a cultural landscape by its users. The essential difference between untouched wilderness and other types of landscape is that the latter is always culturally transformed to some degree. In terms of a local community, a place can take on the character of 'a community of memory', in Josiah Royce's phrase.[21] The landscape becomes a physical realization of that community. Just as it is a commonplace to note that a garden is often an expression of the owner's personality, it can also be true that a landscape is a reflection of the community that interacts with it. Albert Camus put it like this: 'Sense of place is not just something people know and feel, it is something people do'.[22] These are not uncontroversial statements when one considers the architectural development of cities and their neighbourhoods – it is a leitmotif of Peter Ackroyd's *London*, for example. A city can seem to speak to us quite distinctly, as Louis Kahn suggests: 'A city is a place where a small boy, as he walks through it, may see something that will tell him what he wants to do with his whole life.'[23] In other words, a city is better than a landscape at communicating with us, perhaps because in the city the level of human interaction with place is lived at a more intense pitch. It is analogous to the old stereotype of rural taciturnity and urban sophistication.

The mediation is more subtle in landscapes and gardens than it is in cities. Heidegger describes art as existing in terms both of the creator and of 'a people's historical existence',[24] and the same is true of designed spaces. In this situation, human memory contains both an idea of community memory – 'the sense of sharing the features and aura of a particular place with its earlier inhabitants'[25] – and personal memory of the place after repeated visits. Our memories of places are in fact just as meaningful and resonant as our direct, real-time experiences of them, and that is part of the secret power of a community's interaction with places: people arrive fully loaded, as it were.

If, as E. Walter suggests, 'A place binds people together by the common emotions it elicits',[26] we might extenuate that a place gradually fulfils its meaning or destiny as more people visit it. Its incarnation is self-fulfilling and predetermined, in that it is mutated by commonalities of human experience and emotion, which become absorbed into the fabric of the land in a communal act of co-creation – feeling and doing simultaneously. Alternatively, it could be suggested that the communal or public landscape is subject to what are usually tiny mutations that arise as a result of the interactions of each and every visitor, and that the impact of these mutations varies according to the level or richness of the interchange. This observation admits of the fact that not all places are equally valuable to us, and not all places have equal meaning. The obvious example of a deep relationship with place is that of the owner or custodian of a garden, whose presence so often seems tangibly to fill up the space.

Related to the idea of community or shared memory is the explication of places in literature, and its absorption into the

culture. This is relevant because there is an established pantheon
of great gardens; more than with any other art form, the culture
of landscapes and gardens is a culture of visiting. So many of us
visit gardens after we have read about them, or have heard about
them, thought about them, or even dreamt about them over a
number of years. Seamus Heaney has described the literary
aspect of the sense of place with reference to Ireland:

> As we pass south along the coast from Tory to Knocknarea, we
> go through the village of Drumcliff and under Ben Bulben, we
> skirt Lissadell and Innisfree. All of these places now live in the
> imagination, all of them stir us to responses other than the
> merely visual, all of them are instinct with the poet and his
> poetry. Irrespective of our creed or politics, irrespective of
> what culture or subculture may have coloured our individual
> sensibilities, our imaginations assent to the stimulus of names,
> our sense of place is enhanced, our sense of ourselves as
> inhabitants not just of a geographical country but of a country
> of the mind is cemented. It is this feeling, assenting, equable
> marriage between the geographical country and the country
> of the mind, whether that country of the mind takes its tone
> unconsciously from a shared oral inherited culture, or from a
> consciously savoured literary culture, or from both, it is this
> marriage that constitutes the sense of place in its richest pos-
> sible manifestation. [27]

On a personal, individual level, the most intimate relationship
one can have as co-creator of a garden or landscape is as an
owner. It is here that our personalities and cultural motivations
become most apparent. Over the years one's character seems to
seep into the space. As Freya Stark put it: 'This surely is the
meaning of home – a place where every day is multiplied by all
the days before it.'[28] The garden is a part of the home, and as such
it is often a foundation of identity. We put down roots – emotional and horticultural. Merleau-Ponty said of Cézanne that the

work of art is not simply the product of the artist. It is the artist's manner of existing and his source of life. In the case of gardens, that is often palpably true. The importance of the home in the domestic sense, and of the locale one identifies as 'home', is evinced by the extreme distress of people displaced by war and other disasters. There are many cases of people admitting to more shock at the destruction of their home, village or city, than to the deaths of their fellow citizens.

For many gardeners, the exterior areas of the home are even more meaningful than the interiors, because gardening is a pastime and it is necessary to have an (almost) daily relationship with the place, subject to the vagaries of weather, season and personal whim. A garden can be an expression of solidarity between two lovers, but it is a fact that many people have a more meaningful relationship with their garden than they do with their spouse or partner. The idea of being in the 'right place', of finding a situation where one feels comfortable and somehow right, can relate to a role such as motherhood, or to a job or vocation. For others it can be a physical place on whatever scale, whether it is a small garden, or a shed, or the whole of the ocean – round-the-world yachtswoman Ellen MacArthur described the world's oceans, her destiny, as 'a place', singular. When you find an occupation, such as gardening, that is also a physical place, and you put more and more of yourself into it, you become conjoined with it, subsumed in it. It seems to become part of you and you seem to become part of it. And that is the root of many of the best domestic gardens.

Arnold Berleant has summarized the importance of place in our lives: 'For most people, the lived, living landscape is the commonplace setting of everyday life, and how we engage with the prosaic landscapes of home, work, local travel and recreation is an important measure of the quality of our lives. How we engage aesthetically with our landscape is a measure of the intrinsic value of our experience.'[29] In aesthetic terms, simply being outdoors creates a completely different spatial, emotional, cultural and artistic context. There are so many variables and distractions. In one sense, nature is chaos. Landscapes and gardens are places where we might have what feels like a visceral, emotional, almost unmediated interaction with the world of raw experience. Compare our experience of physical engagement with a garden with the quotidian realities of a life lived mainly indoors, where we travel around in cars – in our own private bubbles – and segue from one carefully ordered (and generally predictable) indoor space to the next. Outside, we are physically and emotionally vulnerable, and therefore more sensitive to our surroundings. Our effortless engagement with the landscape that surrounds us outdoors is in its way as intense an engagement as the one we effortfully invent when considering a painting or sculpture in the art gallery, though by its nature it is often more diffuse.

Central to gardens and landscapes is the sense of physical, bodily engagement that is common to both owner-gardeners and visitors. For Whitehead, this idea of the body subsumed into the universe is central to our experience: 'The body is part of the external world, continuous with it. In fact, it is just as much part of nature as anything else there – a river, or a mountain, or a cloud. Also, if we are fussily exact, we cannot define where a body begins and where external nature ends.'[30] This feeling of participation with nature chimes uniquely with the innate mutability of gardens and the general view of the universe espoused by Whitehead: 'For the modern view, process, activity and change are the matter of fact. At an instant there is nothing. Each instant is only a way of grouping matters of fact. Thus, since there are no instants, conceived as simple primary entities, there is no Nature at an instant. Thus, all the interrelations of matters of fact must involve transition in their essence. All realization involves implication in the creative advance.'[31] If one takes Whitehead's point seriously, the act of gardening can be viewed as a living paradigm of this philosophy of the never-ending process of experiencing: it is an interaction with the world that honours the idea of transition and the creative advance of all matter and experience.

The interconnectedness of the mind of place and the mind of a human is also discussed in the work of the pioneer child psychologist Jean Piaget, who maintained that 'the true nature of space does not reside in the more or less extended character of sensations as such, but in the intelligence which interconnects these sensations'.[32] We are collaborators, not observers, and if we do indeed imaginatively co-create the spaces around us, our mental interactions must also influence their nature.

This idea of a co-mingling of the human mind with the 'mind' of a place leads to the realization that when both parties emerge from the process, each has been transformed to some extent – although in most cases, the change in the human is far more marked and easily verifiable (through conversation). Landscapes cannot speak to us in that way, of course (although Mickey Mouse's house in Disneyland, which is filled with Mickey's disembodied voice, does seem to be able to). How, then, to discern the effects of human minds on place-minds? If we can all agree that someone who actively gardens a space has a real and lasting effect on it, and that that effect is not purely physical in its nature, is it not therefore reasonable to suggest that someone else who lives at that address, who does not garden themselves but who uses the garden regularly, also has some lasting impact on it? And is it not therefore also true that someone who visits the garden on just one occasion will also have some effect on it, even if it is infinitesimal, which may or may not be discernible to another visitor in the future? That is what co-creation is all about. It is certainly true that if someone famous visits a garden even fleetingly, that garden can be materially affected forever. I remember visiting one north London garden where the owners were touchingly proud that the actress Maureen Lipman, an enthusiastic visitor on an open day, had become a friend and described it as her favourite garden. The influence of celebrity there was tangible (and honest), even though it had resulted from just a few visits. This is an example of a garden being deeply and lastingly affected by a visitor in a non-physical way – for the owner, at least. Perhaps a more marked example of co-creation is the way gardens change when they are opened to the public on rare occasions, for instance as part of the National Gardens Scheme. Ask anyone who opens their garden for the NGS whether the atmosphere of their garden (and not just the state of the grass) has changed when all the people have gone home. It almost always has; in some cases, it has been altered forever.

How does this process of co-creation, of 'mind gardening', actually work? Berleant describes the process of co-creation as a fusion of mind and place:

> An evocative landscape, rich with interest and detail, may be absorbing but is still incomplete; it requires our thoughts, associations, knowledge and responses. If an active interpenetration of person and place develops, a fusion may emerge that depends on our personal contribution, on how we activate the environment by engaging with its features and bringing them into meaningful juxtaposition with our memories and associations. When this fusion occurs with focus and intensity, the experience may acquire the peculiar yet charmed humility we associate with the sacred.[33]

Although it introduces the concept of the activation of the environment, this reading stops short of psychotopia: a description of co-creation as an actual experience that is lived in the world, by both place and person. Instead it appeals to the notion of sacredness. The argument owes something to the specificities of Heidegger's influential 1951 lecture, 'Building Dwelling Thinking', which introduced his concept of the fourfold of earth, sky, mortals and divinities. The fourfold defines what it really means to dwell (in this context, simply 'to be') on Earth.

'When places are actively sensed,' Heidegger said, 'the physical landscape becomes wedded to the landscape of the mind, to the roving imagination, and where the mind may lead is anybody's guess.' It is a visionary explication of a dynamic process, although Heidegger also sees building, dwelling and thinking as a desirable human prerogative, in that dwelling is understanding our place in the cosmos, building is expressing those ideals, and thinking is our awareness of it.

Perhaps the most physicalized description of the process of co-creation is Jean-Paul Sartre's discussion of the affective state of objects:

> When knowledge and feeling are oriented towards something real, actually perceived, the thing, like a reflector, returns the light it has received from it. As a result of this continual inter-action, meaning is continually enriched at the same time as the object soaks up affective qualities. The object thus obtains its own particular depth and richness. The affective state flows [with] the progress of attention, developing with each new discovery of meaning . . . with the result that its development is unpredictable. At each moment perception overflows it and sustains it, and its density and depth come from its being con-fused with the perceived object. Each quality is so deeply incorporated in the object that it is impossible to distinguish what is felt and what is perceived.[34]

This is what happens with landscapes and gardens: when we are there, we experience an intense interaction as co-creators, and the place generates its own field of meaning.

It is quite possible for a person to continue to actively co-cre-ate a landscape after death. This process is allied to the notion of co-creativity in absentia that we have seen at work in the case of celebrities. Think of any well-known garden – Sissinghurst or Giverny, perhaps – and the sense of influence from beyond the grave becomes self-evident. This is not to say, incidentally, that our ideas about the character, aims and motivations of these deceased individuals are in any way based in actual fact or real experience, communicated to us in detail through some spiritual hotline; it is just that our ideas about the absent creators materially affect our personal engagement with the garden. We do not only discern, but also invent our spiritual links with those who made the garden many years before. To ignore these ambiguous factors in our experience would be to engage dishonestly with the life of the garden.

COSMIC RELATIONSHIP: TIME AND PLACE

The psychic connection between people and place may not simply be emotional but hold greater significance for us. Some of our worries about what a landscape or garden is – is it a space, or an object, or an experience? – mirror our concerns about our relationship with the cosmos.

The importance of place was appreciated by Aristotle, who included 'where' as one of the ten defining characteristics of any object. But in Newtonian physics, place became just another way of describing the physical compartmentalization of space: in this reading, space is by definition empty and has no specific properties of its own. In recent years a few philosophers and scientists have tried to reclaim place as a defining aspect of humanity – as more important than time, for example. A radical idea has been floated (by Heidegger) that space and time are contained in places rather than places in them. This idea of place as the beginning of all experience has gained currency in recent years. In a recent essay the philosopher Edward S. Casey even suggested that the phenomenological 'lifeworld' be replaced by 'place-world'.[35]

Cosmologists have now given up on the idea of the linear progression of history through time, in favour of a view of the cosmos defined by the types of raw energies it contains. Time has been discredited: it varies from the top of a tall building to the bottom, time runs differently in space, and in any case the human conception of time is fatally biased towards the future. Perhaps we do not live 'in time', after all, because we do not understand infinity, rather we live in places, in the where, which we can more readily comprehend. Everything we do and perceive has to happen in some place. We cannot imagine time without place, and when we do, we call it limbo, or hell. But you can have place without time. I would suggest that a date in the diary is more of a place than a time.

In this respect, mainstream science seems finally to have caught up with Whitehead. In a rare flash of vivid prose in *Process and Reality*, Whitehead defined the way that the profound essences experienced in life endure through time through the example of a singular work of art:

> In the inescapable flux, there is something that abides; in the overwhelming permanence, there is an element that escapes into flux. Permanence can be snatched only out of flux; and the passing moment can find its adequate intensity only by its submission to permanence. Those who would disjoin the two elements can find no interpretation of patent facts. The four symbolic figures in the Medici chapel in Florence – Michelangelo's masterpieces of statuary, Day and Night, Evening and Dawn – exhibit the everlasting elements in the passage of fact. The figures stay there, reclining in their recurring sequence, forever showing the essences in the nature of things. The perfect realisation is not merely the exemplification of what in abstraction is timeless. It does more: it implants timelessness on what in its essence is passing. The perfect moment is fadeless in the lapse of time. Time has then lost its character of 'perpetual perishing'; it becomes the 'moving image of eternity'.[36]

This 'perfect moment . . . fadeless in the lapse of time', embodied in the sculptures, is emblematic of the enduring value of aesthetic experience across all media. It is not the personal moment of epiphany described by Joyce and the Modernists, but something with larger significance.

The perfect moment may indeed endure, but of what does it consist for the individual? What are we to make of all those swirling mental associations that tumble around us? In 1967 Michel Foucault gave a lecture in which he introduced some potentially useful imagery: 'The present epoch will perhaps be above all the epoch of space. We are in the epoch of simultaneity; we are in the epoch of juxtaposition, the epoch of the near and far, of the side-by-side, of the dispersed. We are at a moment, I believe, when our experience of the world is less that of a long life developing through time than that of a network that connects points and intersects with its own skein.'[37]

In this world throbbing with meaning, each place is a matrix of energy that is connected with thousands of others in our memories. Places are the interconnecting nodes of our experience. It is akin to a London taxi driver's 'knowledge': they do not carry a whole map of the city about in their head, but a series of little vignettes of places which they connect up together as they go. They feel their way as they drive around. We could think of our consciousness as thousands of such 'knowledges': A to Zs of friends, food preferences, the weather, foreign countries, and so on.

If places are the interconnecting nodes of our experience, a spatial plane which is perhaps more important than the temporal in terms of our relationship with the universe, then this must have a bearing on our attitude to death. We tend to think of death as the end of a life lived through time, and imagine that what we fear about death is the sudden extinction of that life. But perhaps this fundamental fear of death is founded not in anticipation of the absence of life, but in a fear of suddenly being

nowhere. (In our society, the lowest castes of all are the place-
less peoples: the gypsies, the travellers, the refugees, the asylum
seekers.) To be in no place, psychologically speaking, is the
worst fate of all, since it means either madness or death,
whereas to be in a place that is right is paradise – which brings
us back to our beloved gardens.

Garden and landscape design is the aesthetic correlative of
this meaningful relationship with the universe. All places are
matrices of energy where thousands of strands of meaning
enwrap and enfold the visitor, who also becomes a participant
and co-creator of that place. Our gardens are, for many of us, the
most special places of all, filled with myriad threads of experience, emotion and memory, which make our gardens meaningful. The sense of place that arises from this profound interaction
between humanity and nature transcends not just the physical
world, but even time itself. That is why garden and landscape art
is so special: it is the only art form which not only transcends
time, by working alongside it, but also grapples with and
attempts to manipulate the sense of place, the psychotopia.
Sculpture and the plastic arts seem limited by comparison. This
lack of artistic control is anathema to most artists, for whom the
landscape is all too often simply a setting for an art object, but
the mutability and changing nature of landscape gives it a kind of
state of grace of the present.

There is a beautiful paradox at the heart of landscapes and
gardens. In one sense, gardens are clearly at the mercy of time –
in the shape of the seasons and the passage of the day. They
change continually. But this enslavement to the movements of
the sun and moon also imbues them with a tangible timelessness.
Their very mutability instils in them solidity and inspires reverence. In gardens, we tend to look in on ourselves and lose the
idea of time. So although gardens are enslaved by the rules of
daily and seasonal time, they also chime transcendently with cos-
mic time.

We started with the idea of sense of place. It is something that everyone involved with gardens seems to talk about and revere, but no one is able to define. Even those who like to imagine that their relationship with the world is sturdily rational – that all experience is reducible to cultural context – find themselves admitting of the existence of something more in terms of life as it is lived. Psychotopia represents a descriptive attitude to be used for examining what it is in experience that makes places seem special or unique to us, taking into account both observable facts and more abstract intuitions. This essay is based on the practical premise that if we know what something is, or at least have a way of talking about it, we might be able to appreciate it in greater depth – and perhaps even manipulate it better. So this has been a practical gardening column, of sorts.

NOTES

1. For an attempt to do this see four essays on the subject of place by the present author in *Hortus*, nos 57–60, 2001: 'What Makes a Space a Place?'; 'We See Gardens Not As They Are, But As We Are'; 'The Shape of the Land'; and 'The Ghost in the Garden'.

2. Gaston Bachelard, *The Poetics of Space*, New York, 1964.

3. Arnold Berleant, *The Aesthetics of Environment*, Philadelphia, 1992, chapter 3.

4. 'The Origin of the Work of Art' by Martin Heidegger in his *Poetry, Language, Thought* (translated by Albert Hofstadter), New York, 1971.

5. Quoted in Lev Braun, *Witness of Decline: Albert Camus: Moralist of the Absurd*, Rutherford, 1974, chapter 8.

6. From A.N. Whitehead, *Modes of Thought*, 1938, pp. 202–3, quoted in Ivor Leclerc, *Whitehead's Metaphysics: An Introductory Exposition*, London, 1958, note p. 35.

7. Elizabeth M. Kraus, *The Metaphysics of Experience, A Companion to Whitehead's Process and Reality*, New York, 1998.

8. Edward Relph, *Rational Landscapes and Humanistic Geography*, London, 1981, pp. 171–2.

9. Christian Norberg-Schultz, *Genius Loci*, London, 1980.

10. *Ibid*.

11. Berleant, p. 20.

12. Alfred North Whitehead, *Nature and Life (Two Lectures)*, Cambridge, 1934.

13. Maurice Merleau-Ponty, *Phenomenology of Perception* (translated by Colin Smith), London, 1962.

14. Quoted in Herbert Spiegelberg, *The Phenomenological Movement*, The Hague and London 1982.

15. Mikel Dufrenne, *The Phenomenology of Aesthetic Experience* (translated by Edward S. Casey), Evanston, 1973, p. 79.

16. Christian Norberg-Schultz, *Existence, Space and Architecture*, London, 1971.

17. Berleant, chapter 3.

18. Quoted in John Pickles, *Phenomenology, Science and Geography: Spatiality and the Human Sciences*, Cambridge, 1985, p. 139.

19. James J Gibson, *The Perception of the Visual World*, Cambridge, Mass., 1950.

20. E.H. Gombrich, *Art and Illusion*, London, 1960.

21. Josiah Royce, *The Problem of Christianity*, Chicago, 1913; 1968, pp. 243–8.

22. Albert Camus, *Noces suivi de l'eté*, Paris, 1955, p. 88, quoted in Keith H. Basso, 'Wisdom Sits in Places' in *Senses of Place*, edited by Basso and Steven Feld, Santa Fe, 1996.

23. Quoted in Norberg-Schultz, *Existence, Space and Architecture*.

24. 'The Origin of the Work of Art' by Martin Heidegger in his *Poetry, Language, Thought* (translated by Albert Hofstadter), New York, 1971, pp. 17–87.

25. Berleant, *The Aesthetics of Environment*.

26. Eugene Victor Walter, *Placeways: A Theory of the Human Environment*, Chapel Hill and London 1988.

27. 'The Sense of Place', a lecture given in 1977, Seamus Heaney, *Preoccupations: Selected Prose 1968–1978*, London, 1980.

28. Quoted in Yi-Fu Tuan, *Topophilia: A Study of Environmental Perception, Attitudes and Values*, Engelwood Cliffs, 1974.

29. Arnold Berleant, *Living in the Landscape: Towards an Aesthetics of Environment*, Lawrence, 1997.

30. From A.N. Whitehead, *Modes of Thought*, 1938, pp. 29–30, quoted in Ivor Leclerc, *Whitehead's Metaphysics: An Introductory Exposition*, London, 1958, p. 131.

31. Whitehead, *Nature and Life (Two Lectures)*.

32. Jean Piaget, *The Child's Construction of Reality*, 1955, quoted in Christian Norberg-Schultz, *Existence, Space and Architecture*, London, 1971.

33. Berleant, *Living in the Landscape*, p. 170.

34. From *The Philosophy of Jean-Paul Sartre*, edited by R. Cumming, New York, 1965, quoted in Keith H. Basso, 'Wisdom Sits in Places' in *Senses of Place*, edited by Basso and Steven Feld, Santa Fe, 1996.

35. Edward S. Casey, 'Smooth Spaces and Rough-Edged Places: The Hidden History of Place', available at webpage: www.sunysb.edu/philosophy/faculty/ecasey.html.

36. Alfred North Whitehead, *Process and Reality*, Cambridge, 1929.

37. A 1967 lecture called 'Of Other Spaces' reprinted in *Diacritics*, spring 1986 vol. 16, no. 1.

NYC WTC 9/11
The Healing Gardens of Paradise Lost

Lorna McNeur

The author, a native New Yorker, explores some of the complex cultural and symbolic issues surrounding the development of Manhattan's landscape and grid, and discusses how things changed after 9/11.

> Death is a part of life, just as winter is a part of spring . . .
> death means change. We can't expect one gift from the
> Creator without accepting the other. We can't live forever, or
> prevent anything from changing. We can only prepare our-
> selves for change. Nevertheless, it is tragic that so many who
> had so much to share with the world died so quickly . . .[1]

Following the destruction of the World Trade Center, these haunting words hold as true today as they did for the Native Americans when they were written about 350 years ago, following the desecration of their people, land and culture on Manhattan island, on the same soil as the Lower Manhattan Financial District, location of 'Ground Zero'.

In this text, I explore transformations in the Manhattan landscape. Beginning with the once-sacred island of the ancient Native New Yorkers, through the battles for land and life between the Native New Yorkers and the European Settlers, I then look at the gridding of the landscape and erasure of natural conditions. Investigating the messages emitted and the quality of life ensuing in the midst of a productivity- and efficiency-minded gridded urban landscape, I then discuss the essence of this urban-scape ethos as it was embodied in the World Trade Center. Throughout, I am looking at the imbalances that can occur when

there is superimposition rather than integration and appreciation
for the interrelationships between culture, politics, landscape
and lives. I conclude by making proposals for green public space
throughout the city, based on an understanding of the soul of the
city.

ANCIENT NATIVE NEW YORKERS
Manhattan Island and Paradise Lost

There are many historical documents written about Manhattan
as an island of paradise that was once sacred to New York's
Native Americans, who I refer to in this text as the ancient
Native New Yorkers, to make both the connection and distinction with contemporary Native New Yorkers. In his book, *Native
New Yorkers*, Evan Pritchard tells us that for at least one thousand
years before the seventeenth-century European occupation, the
'Real People' of the Manhattan Lenape tribe (a tribe of the
Algonquin nation), 'lived in a beautiful garden like paradise surrounding what is now called New York Harbor. They were well
aware of their destructive potential as human beings, and strove
to interact gracefully with their environment and humans without causing permanent damage whenever possible.'[2]

Prior to European contact, there were Algonquin farming
communities with highly developed farming methods that
assumed deep respect for the land and were in harmony with the
seasons and nature's cycles. There was well-drained soil and
good water; planting, hunting, fishing in the Spring; wild flowers
perfuming the air; and travelling for trade and adventure.
Manhattan was a meeting place to 'exchange goods, share knowledge, give thanks, and show respect to the Spirits. When the
leaves changed colour, there was harvesting, hunting and collecting of food for the winter. During the cold moons of long nights
they made objects for trade, repaired tools, told lesson stories,
and celebrated festivals.'[3] Johannes de Laet, one of the first

Dutch historians to describe the region, wrote in 1626, 'The land is excellent and agreeable, full of noble forests, trees, and grapevines. [Working it well will] render it one of the finest and most fruitful lands in that part of the world.'[4]

Pritchard also tells us that the Lenape tribe had long established the 'great trading center' in what would become the Wall Street area. 'The southern tip of Manhattan . . . was a well-known trading spot. Goods were plentiful, and fur traders travelled from hundreds of miles around to make deals there.'[5] Following on from this, the first European trading post was established in Lower Manhattan in 1613, just a few blocks from what was to become the World Trade Center site.

ARRIVAL OF THE EUROPEAN SETTLERS

The arrival of the white men was foretold by the elders at least one year in advance. With anticipation the Native Americans waited, not quite knowing whether the arrival would be a blessing or otherwise. However, they were prepared to greet who they thought might be the gods from the east, coming from the direction of the sun, and to welcome them warmly and generously, offering food, clothing, hospitality and land. However, once they arrived, over a period of time it became painfully clear that the agendas of the clashing cultures were worlds apart.

Wars waged on the Native Americans by the white settlers aimed at annihilation. Thousands of Native American men, women and children lost their lives, history, culture, land and spirit – all on the soil that is the foundation of the city of New York. In 1647, one of the worst massacres on North American soil took place at Pound Ridge, New York, and was carried out with religious zeal with one account stating that 'the scripture declareth women and children must perish with their parents'.[6] This single story epitomises much of the Native American experience of genocide and devastation.

Between five and seven hundred Algonquin were ambushed and killed as they were gathering for the important spiritual celebration k'mo'hok ki'coy or 'hungry moon', often called Maple Sugar Dance. Arriving at midnight at Pound Ridge on foot, the white colonists (some say 200 of them, some 130) found three rows of well-constructed houses, each seventy paces long (some say eighty), made of square logs. One hundred eighty Lenape came outside to see what the noise was and were killed where they stood outside the houses. Others tried to escape but were driven back into the houses. General Montagne gave the order to burn them inside the houses. Soon the many long houses were torched. Eight men escaped. The people inside preferred to die by fire than be killed by whites, so they sat inside and didn't make a single sound. Not one Lenape among the many hundreds who were burned alive screamed.[7]

In speaking of the councils of Native American wisdom teachers, Pritchard explains that, 'The ashes of those council fires are still buried beneath the New York streets, the bones of those saints still rest encased by cement. All of them spoke of the earth as if she were their own mother.'[8] And 'the spirits of the Native American Land Keepers still keep silent watch over the terrain.'[9]

NATURE AND THE GRID-PLAN LAYOUT OF NEW YORK

Over the succeeding centuries, New York developed rapidly and successfully established itself as an international urban centre. In the early nineteenth century, three commissioners were assigned the task of establishing a layout for the fast growing city. In their highly pragmatic approach they operated as economists and traffic engineers, reducing the potential richness of New York to a minimal instrumental structure, promoting efficiency and productivity. While this solution may have met the requirements of the city as an urban system it failed to address the multitude of needs relating to levels of human interaction of a social, cultural, political and spiritual nature.

The superimposition of the gridded street plan on to Manhattan island led to the levelling of the landscape, with little consideration for the existing hills, valleys, rocky outcrops, cliffs, overlooks, ponds, hamlets and farmsteads, thus eliminating rich possibilities for reciprocity between urban topography and natural geography. The abstract character of the grid creates a self-referentially human-made world in which the inhabitants experience minimal contact with nature. For those New Yorkers connected to the city as a machine, the continuity of the seasons is rarely acknowledged, except in severe weather conditions like snow storms, hurricanes and heat waves when nature is experienced more as an inconvenience and a disruption to productivity, rather than appreciated for its replenishing qualities.

Like busy beavers, the business (busyness) of the commercial world disconnects people from natural conditions, causing both harm to themselves and other living beings and plants around them. There is an old Algonquin story that tells of the industriousness of beavers and their busy goal-oriented way of cutting down all the trees. Their obsessive work ignores the existing ecosystem so much that they leave no trees for birds to nest, there is no shade, and all the other animals are unhappy. Losing touch with the natural world around us can have devastating effects, not only for ourselves, but also for all people, plants and animals.

DEMOCRACY AND THE GRID

The grid street system first appeared in Greek antiquity, representing a democratic mapping of the city because it set out a fair and equal block and street structure. Additionally, the grid was orientated according to the four directions of north, south, east and west, thus assuring success and longevity for the city because it was connected into the larger cosmological order. However, the role of the grid in contemporary society concerns the logistics of commercial productivity as a mechanism of machine-minded efficiency.

In theory, the grid can promote democracy by nullifying particularly advantageous natural conditions, giving equal opportunity to all and privileging none. By levelling nature, literally and metaphorically, to an undifferentiated and homogenous state, it allegedly levels the classes by giving the majority of people more equal starting points. However, to the Native Americans, erasure of topography was synonymous with cultural and racial genocide. Manhattan island, once a beautiful 'island of paradise' for its native inhabitants, is now a dense, urban, gridiron city. Frederick Law Olmsted, the architect of Central Park, wrote disdainfully about the grid in 1877:

> Some two thousand blocks were provided, each theoretically two hundred feet wide, no more no less; and ever since, if a building site is wanted, whether with a view to a church or a blast furnace, an open house or a toy shop, there is, of intention, no better place in one of these blocks than an other . . . The clerk or mechanic and his young family . . . is provided for in this respect not otherwise than the wealthy merchant . . .[10]

Here is democracy taken to its extreme. The creation of equal spaces, represented by the grid, required the elimination of special places. With the natural conditions of the undulating hills and valleys erased, the buildings became the reference points, thus reinforcing the self-referential nature of this self-contained island city. With nature and history essentially eliminated, a specificity of place was lost with the result that inhabitants were distanced and alienated from their own environment. Here, the grid was not only superimposed over the natural conditions of the island but also on the nature of the lives within it.

Richard Sennet explains that the city grid plan can have pro-
foundly numbing effects on the inhabitants. He writes: 'gridded
space does more than create a blank canvas for development. It
subdues those who must live in the space, disorienting their ability to see and to evaluate relationships. In that sense, the planning of neutral space is an act of dominating and subduing
others.'[11] The very structure of the city breeds a mentality that
can be both highly productive and deeply destructive. The combination of the gridded plan on the finite condition of Manhattan
as an island creates a concentration that engenders a work mentality of the highest order. All of these conditions and many
more, contribute to a competitively hostile environment with
very little time to spare for human frailty, and the tragedies that
arise from such conditions.

The obsession with technology, efficiency and productivity
that has seized society in the past few centuries, has reached its
zenith in international cities like contemporary New York. Such
environments engender patterns of living that are predominantly
diagrammatic. We are born into this and assume it as reality,
rather than choice. This reminds me of an Algonquin children's
story that illustrates how the Lenape felt about the European set-
tlement of their land.

There are many stories about snakes among the Algonquin.
One story tells of two Native American children, a boy and a
girl, who find a harmless little snake . . . wriggling in the forest. They take it home as a pet. They feed it leaves and other
odds and ends, only to find that it grows at an amazing rate.
The more they feed it, the more voracious the snake's
appetite becomes. It eats the dog, then the cat, then all the
surrounding squirrels and rabbits. It even tries to eat the baby,
but is stopped in time. However, from that point on, the boy
and girl are occupied every waking minute with finding meat
for the snake so it won't eat them. The snake turns into a

monster and begins devouring the land and everything on it. It is said that the snake is still alive today, but no one will say what form it has taken.[12]

NYC WTC 9/11

The World Trade Center towers represented, among many things, the essence of New York: financially orientated professions and people encased in gridded vertical 'islands'. Here was the grid taken to its ultimate extreme. Reaching the intellectual heights and structural limits of the abilities of humankind, these two buildings stood as far removed from nature as is humanly possible.

The hard drive of Manhattan was epitomised in the World Trade Center buildings. Every day these buildings were full of people, earnestly 'beavering' away, caught in the wheel of the urban machine that we all take for granted as reality. In order to support our lifestyles we have to earn more and more, taking precious time away from family and friends. Working to live has become living to work.

The underlying ethos and normal mode of operation of New York City has been crisis management. This machine-minded city ground to a halt on September 11, 2001, now referred to as 9/11, the same number as the United States crisis phone number for emergency services, 911. This was the day that New York was thrust upon the world stage, in its moment of ultimate crisis.

Death always puts life into perspective. 9/11 put life into perspective for New Yorkers on a multitude of levels. Only something as huge as this could stop in its tracks the larger-than-life urban machine that is New York. After experiencing the destruction of buildings, lives and families on 9/11, millions of New Yorkers have reassessed the quality of their lives. Many have moved out of the city to bring up their children in a more forgiving, nourishing environment, simultaneously changing lifestyles, attitudes and expectations.

September 11 has changed significantly the nature of daily life within the city as well. In 2003, two years after the attack, the after-effects were still extremely noticeable. Pedestrians were not fighting frantically for survival amongst the heavy flowing river of yellow cabs, delivery trucks and cars that ruled the city. What was once taken for granted (the traffic seemed as permanent as the buildings) had been significantly reduced, and pedestrians could relax. They could breathe more easily, literally and metaphorically.

The lower frequency of noise, movement and frustration meant that it was safer to experience being in the environment, rather than constantly racing through it. There was not the usual rushing about from pillar to post, creating a frenetic, fast-paced environment that was baffling but exhilarating to people visiting the city from afar. New Yorkers were actually walking, even strolling! They seemed to be more present in their environment and were absorbing their experience of it, rather than constantly escaping it, through rushing.

Was the World Trade Center disaster New York's healing crisis? Have we all been caught in a machine so large that it took an equally huge tragic force to stop it and make us see the senselessness of the lives that we have been living? The film *Koyaanisqatsi* (a Native American term meaning 'life out of balance') prophetically portrays this phenomenon.

The foundations of the Manhattan Financial District were built in sacred soil and on the tragic misfortunes of others, rising ever higher above the ashes of the ancient Native New Yorkers. Is it really wise to build ever higher again, this time on the ashes of contemporary metropolitan martyrs? What has been learned from the tragic events of 9/11? What have we learned from the fall of these two mighty oaks of civilization?

There is a famous Cree saying that expresses the way many Munsee, and Native Americans in general, feel about what has become of their island, Manhattan: 'Only after the last tree has been cut down, only after the last river has been poisoned, only after the last fish has been caught, only then will you find that money cannot be eaten.'[13]

FOREST FOR THE TREES IN PARADISE LOST

Precious few trees and public spaces exist on the grid-locked island of Manhattan. For the puritanical mindset of the early nineteenth-century commissioners, the words 'public space' and 'loitering' were synonymous in an environment that assumed work and success as its highest priority. However, in the aftermath of 9/11, New Yorkers are discovering that the few urban piazzas and squares that they do have are welcome restful places; not only contrasting and complementing the preconditioned structure of the city grid but also offering solace to an entire city suffering the after-effects of devastating trauma. The New York Public Library gardens are brim-full with lunchtime office workers, and easily overheard conversations between tables find the words '9/11' crop up at almost every third table.

Carl Schorske evokes the beliefs of the Austrian architect and town planner Camillo Sitte in his hope for the return of street life when he writes: 'In the cold, traffic swept modern city of the slide-rule and the slum, the picturesque comforting square can reawaken memories of the vanished Burgher past. This spatially dramatic memory will inspire us to create a better future, free of philistinism and utilitarianism.'[14]

Green urban spaces are places where people can express and celebrate their humanity in all its diversity. Without spaces like these, human beings are denied their individuality and creativity and the opportunity to connect with others on a multitude of levels ranging from the quietly intimate to the international;

from contemplations or conversations in the company of others to international cultural celebrations and political demonstrations.

The gridded road pattern has left too few squares and parks to meet the needs of the millions of inhabitants who could be benefiting from the presence of urban public spaces of reflection and replenishment. Central Park does provide for this need in New York but its location hinders its ability to do so for all. Nevertheless, this grand green space contains clues to places for green public space to be integrated elsewhere into the existing fabric of New York City.

CENTRAL PARK AND BROADWAY
Prevailing Spirits of Native New York

Central Park

Central Park is an oasis in an otherwise mechanistic environment. It is an island of nature, a green reservoir in the centre of the city, of the island of Manhattan. The park plays its role in softening the many tragedies of urban life and offers respite for those who cannot afford to leave the city. Paradoxically, one turns inward to the centre of the city to escape the urban intensity. Here is a landscape designed to protect the citizens from their own urban environment.

We have seen that, rather than creating a cityscape that integrated some natural conditions, the city was levelled and gridded. In the centre a rectangle of space for a park was retained as a way of counteracting some of the consciously perceived negative effects that the grid would have on daily living. It is ironic that the grid destroyed the majority of the landscape of the island but the remaining area in the centre was encased as a gem within a rectangle of space, an island of green within the gridded urbanscape. However, despite the democratic intentions of being centrally located and therefore accessible to all, in practice, Central

Park has proved to be too far away for most city dwellers to reach in their daily routines. One large space in the centre of a huge city primarily serves those who live or work around it, whilst others must simply do without. Other than Central Park, Manhattan offers surprisingly few public spaces for rest and replenishment, amidst the high-stress New York world of urban intensity. For the sanity and dignity of the whole city, integrated public space throughout is essential.

The landscape architect Frederick Law Olmsted began the design of the park in 1850 by organizing the park's major road systems according to the overall road structure of New York.[15] A formal analysis of the plan of Central Park reveals some striking parallels between the park and the city:[16]

1. Manhattan is a long and thin island with proportions of 1:5. Central Park is a long and thin 'green island' with proportions of 1:5.

2. Broadway in Manhattan is at a diagonal to the grid, oriented almost due north.
    The Grand Promenade in Central Park is at a diagonal to the grid, oriented almost due north.

3. At the centre of the island of Manhattan is the rectangular 'green lung' reservoir called Central Park.
    At the centre of the 'green island' of Central Park is the rectangular reservoir of water.[17]

In other words, the location of the rectangular reservoir at the centre of Central Park parallels the position of the rectangle of Central Park within Manhattan. In these mirror relationships between the city and the park are lessons to be learned from the park about the city. Ironically, Central Park gives clues to the possibilities for green public space throughout the city that are grounded in the long history of transformation of New York's original landscape, gridded cityscape and park landscape. This progression from the island, to the city, the park, and the reservoir, describes an inward spiralling theme of profound dimensions:

1. The natural island of Manhattan once existed as a sacred green island of paradise.

2. This island was then gridded.

3. In the centre of the gridded island was retained a portion of landscape, Central Park.

4. The plan of Central Park parallels much of the plan of New York City.

5. In the centre of the park was retained a rectangular reservoir (removed in the twentieth century).

Proposal:

> To reinstate the rectangular reservoir in Central Park.
>
> To place into the reservoir, a small-scale version of the original natural island of Manhattan.
>
> To plant this miniature Manhattan with the original seeds of the island and let them grow naturally.

Walking on this island in the heart of Central Park could provide a more tangible sense of Manhattan's paradise lost.

This inward spiralling theme reveals primordial aspects of Manhattan and Central Park. The long and thin island of Manhattan, with the space at the centre, is strikingly anthropomorphic in the sense that it is like a body with a womb at the centre. Metaphorically, the urban inhabitants turn to the sacred oasis of nature at the centre of the city for replenishment and respite from the very world that they have constructed, after destroying the surrounding landscape. The once sacred island of

Manhattan is paradise lost and Central Park is the reinstatement of this lost natural landscape. Central Park is New York's reconstruction of paradise lost.

In other words, the island that was destroyed was then recreated metaphorically in New York's 'garden', Central Park.[18] This interchangeability between garden and city is reinforced by historical notions of paradise, which is referred to simultaneously in both Medieval and Renaissance writings as the Garden of Eden or the Heavenly City.

Another example of this interchangeability between city and garden can be seen in the parallel relationship between the Grand Promenade in Central Park and Broadway in New York:

> The Grand Promenade is the only formal element in the romantic landscape of Central Park.
>
> Broadway is the only large-scale natural condition in the rational grid of New York.

Hence, both the Grand Promenade and Broadway are related as opposites; both are anomalies in their own contexts and both sit at diagonals to the grid.[19]

Broadway – The Grand Promenade

Originating as a Native American trail on the once sacred island of Manhattan, Broadway embodies the stories of both the Native and European inhabitation of the island. Like Central Park, Broadway holds a highly significant place in Manhattan. This is so in its diagonal orientation to the grid as well as its distinctive context as a spine running almost the full length of Manhattan island. As such, Broadway is singular in its orientation, eccentric in its configuration and historical in its age. In contrast to the numbing effects of the grid, the creative spirit of Broadway has always been alive with passion throughout its Native American, European and American history. The history of theatre in New

York is synonymous with Broadway. As the city moved its way up the island, so too did the theatre district make its way up Broadway.

Whether promenading in the park or parading along Broadway, the experience of seeing and being seen is the essence of this urban theatricality. For these reasons and many more, Broadway could easily be described as New York's Grand Promenade. Here again we find the interchangeability between the Grand Promenade of the park and the sacred way of Broadway, in the city. There are six squares along Broadway (Union Square, Madison Square, Greeley Square, Herald Square, Times Square, and Columbus Circle), three of which are actually little more than traffic islands. However, there is great potential for these squares and the length of Broadway to be developed further into integrated green space journeying through the city.

This scale of green space would serve the needs of New Yorkers on many levels: as a calming spirit to ease the turmoil of the recent and distant past and to help to achieve a healthy balance between the active and contemplative experiences of urban living.

HEALING GARDENS IN PARADISE LOST

New York is a much loved and admired international city. Although millions have never been to New York, many feel like they know the city well because of having 'visited' it through a multitude of plays, films, books and television programmes. Indeed, many cities internationally now have numerous towers that together recall the sense of the famous New York skyline. As a high-profile international city, it is no coincidence that the crisis of 9/11 occurred not only in New York but in the World Trade Center.

The twin towers were filled with people from many international cultures and, like New York, these towers were places of interest to millions of family members, friends, colleagues and business associates, the world over. Above and beyond the specific intentions of the terrorists who effected this extraordinary act, there may be a higher agenda than politics and fundamentalist beliefs. Is it possible that what New York has experienced is also an awakening for the rest of the world about how we treat ourselves, each other and the precious planet that we seem to be destroying?

This self-destruct instinct is an ironic phenomenon of humankind. Why is it that we can destroy existing conditions only to subconsciously recreate them on our own terms? We can see this in the destruction of the Manhattan landscape and the recreation of it in Central Park. It can also be seen in the New York urbanscape, where there is an interesting relationship between the geology of the land and the height of the buildings. Manhattan is comprised of granite, primarily, enabling tall towers to be constructed where the depth of stone permits. Consequently, the cityscape mirrors the geology of the landscape in that the towers are tallest and most crowded where the rock is strongest and deepest. The landscape might have been destroyed but the hidden geology of the island inadvertently continues to make its presence known.

Is it too late to try and reconnect with these natural elements and energies that persistently return despite our ability to destroy the very environment that sustains our lives and continuing existence? Do these larger-than-life forces, which seem to be appearing and reappearing in different forms, occur to remind us of what we have lost? These are the sorts of issues that have given rise to the international awareness of the need for a worldwide sustainability agenda.

To quickly rebuild a new World Trade Center tower is akin to simply levelling the island of Manhattan. In other words, quickly rebuilding the World Trade Center towers with what could end up being a token gesture towards a memorial garden at the base and too little regard for the victim's lives, families, friends, and all of the New Yorkers who suffered the 9/11 attack and its after effects, is akin to constructing the rational grid across the Manhattan landscape, with no regard for the lives of the ancient Native New Yorkers, their culture, animals and once beautiful land.

Letting gardens grow on the long-time traumatized island of Manhattan is to let the spirit of the island return to heal the long history of human neglect of both ancient and contemporary Native New Yorkers. Consequently, along with all the other green initiatives already in process, like the Fresh Kills project and others, I propose green public spaces throughout the island of Manhattan in order to gain a healthier balance of active and contemplative spaces throughout the city. The overall proposal would include the World Trade Center site as a memorial garden; Broadway as a green journey through the city, meeting the grand space of Central Park; and the continued development of the perimeter of the island into a string of green public spaces and places.

More specifically, this proposal would include:

1. *World Trade Center Memorial Garden*
The six-storey deep World Trade Center site to be left as a sunken site with cliffs and plateaux for trees and plants to grow upon amidst the exposed granite and soil and for water to collect into a reflective pool or pools at the base. This could be a beautiful garden to either walk into and experience from within or to view from above at street level or further, from the heights of the surrounding buildings. It could prove to be as powerful as the Vietnam War Memorial in Washington that sits embedded in the earth, which has the effect of bringing tears to the eyes of most who visit and read the long list of names of fallen heroes, etched into stone walls.

2. *Broadway as a Green 'Sacred Way'*

With astonishingly few green and/or public spaces integrated throughout the city, Broadway could be developed as a green 'sacred way' for ancient and contemporary Native New Yorkers. This could be a green journey of a promenade with public squares travelling through the city, not only commensurate with the scale of Central Park itself but also leading up through the city and into Central Park. The ancient way of Broadway is New York's truly grand promenade, the sacred way upon which to acknowledge with architectural dignity the joys and sorrows of its inhabitants. This could be a peace offering and memorial to paradise lost, the Native American spirits and the victims of 9/11.

3. *Manhattan Island Perimeter Gardens and Public Spaces*

Manhattan has been rediscovering its waterfront in the past forty years and is still enjoying an awakening to nature in this way. Once-hardened New Yorkers marvel at the sense of freedom and life that they feel as they stroll or roll along the river's edge. The Lower Manhattan Financial District, densely populated within by office buildings and the work-oriented masses that inhabit them, is surrounded on three sides by developing waterfront parks, museums and cafés. Further development could include more river-front piers transformed into sandy urban beaches, and other creative interpretations of urban public space like the elevated highways that have become rollerblading and cycling routes where people can enjoy the breadth of space experienced at the edges of the island. The water's edge around the whole perimeter of Manhattan could be further developed into a sequence of gardens and public spaces acknowledging the elements in ways that New Yorkers rarely afford, celebrating nature and the meeting of the land, the water and the sky.

THE SOUL OF THE CITY

With such little green space throughout, the city can breed and reinforce the hard-nosed mentality commonly associated with New York. But with the introduction of the spirit of hope and life that green spaces and squares can give to urban life, the city's inhabitants would also be given the experience of not only mutual healing for the current aftermath of crisis but could also benefit from the sustaining spirit that the presence of nature brings in urban replenishing spaces.

This is a precious moment in time when the wounds of the past have met those of the present, exposing the rocky cliffs, deep soil, and soul of the city, in the World Trade Center site. This is a rare opportunity for the acknowledgement of the spirit of the island and the people who have lost their lives tragically in the past and present. We are all learning this the hardest way possible and the World Trade Center victims are metropolitan martyrs whose lives were stolen in the process of these painful lessons.

Allowing a garden to grow in the depths of the World Trade Center site would symbolically represent the growth and healing so deeply needed for New Yorkers to return to levels of human health so necessary in an unforgiving urban environment. Daniel Libeskind's tower design proposal, which includes the incorporation of the World Trade Center excavation site as a memorial garden, comes closest to a respectful integration of commercial concerns and meaningful issues. Healing gardens and public spaces throughout New York could contribute to the creation of an environment that encourages continued interaction between peoples, time, and spirit of place, celebrating the beauty of so many different cultures in the deeply rich world of New York City.

NOTES

1. Evan T. Pritchard, *Native New Yorkers, The Legacy of the Algonquin People of New York*, Council Oak, 2003, p. 143.

2. *Ibid.*, p. 17.

3. *Ibid.*, p. 37.

4. *Ibid.*, p. 38.

5. *Ibid.*, p. 174.

6. *Ibid.*, p. 166.

7. *Ibid.*, pp. 166–67.

8. *Ibid.*, p. 51.

9. *Ibid.*, p. 23.

10. Albert Fein, *Fredrick Law Olmsted, Landscape into Cityscape*, (from the Olmsted and Croes document of 1877), New York, 1968.

11. Richard Sennett, *The Conscience of the Eye, The Design and Social Life of Cities*, New York, 1990, p. 60.

12. Pritchard, p.155.

13. *Ibid.*, p. 42.

14. Sennett, p.176.

15. Olmsted writes in his section entitled 'The System of Walks and Rides' within Central Park, that 'it must be necessary to lay out all the principal drives, rides and walks of the Park in lines having a continuous northerly and southerly course, nearly parallel with each other and with the avenues of the city . . .' *Forty Years of Landscape Architecture*, Cambridge, Mass., 1973, p. 378. See also, Charles Capen McLaughlin (ed.), *The Papers of Frederick Law Olmsted, Volume III, Creating Central Park, 1857–1861*, Baltimore, 1983.

16. For a full description of the Central Park analysis that reveals the plan of New York City embedded within Central Park, see L. McNeur, 'Central Park City', the AA Files no. 23, July 1992.

17. This rectangular reservoir existed before Olmsted came to the site and he chose not to remove it from his design.

18. The English landscape design of Central Park is made to appear to be a natural (romantic) landscape, but is, of course, 'artificial nature'.

19. Broadway and the Grand Promenade are both oriented about 3 degrees off due north.

WHERE HAVE ALL THE CRITICS GONE?

Anne Wareham

This powerful polemic is directed at unambitious garden writers, unengaged garden owners and timid garden editors on magazines and newspapers. The author calls for a sea change in our attitudes to gardens, and a sharpening up of the discourse.

I would like to see more great gardens. I think they would enrich our culture. You can express things through the use of land, water and plants that no other art form provides scope for, especially because time and weather are inevitable and dynamic partners in the process. This combination of natural forces and our work upon them has immense resonance, echoing our work in making a living on this planet in partnership with the land.

A great garden requires a site and a person willing and able to transform that site. In order to do that they have to have time, sensitivity, imagination, courage, taste, ruthlessness, a spatial sense and response to pattern, and an ability to learn, especially about their own limitations. And it requires a culture that takes gardens more seriously than we do. We need garden critics and garden criticism. No art can thrive without the serious discussion and dialogue which criticism offers: it raises standards, informs, educates and promotes intelligent debate. It is the lifeblood of any high art, and our gardens are suffering for lack of it. I am not referring here to the garden where the kids play football or that which is devoted to a collection of special plants: I am referring to gardens that open to the public for money.

I think it is possible that the dual sense of the word criticism creates a problem. The dictionary clarifies the ambiguity:

Criticism: 1.the act or an instance of making an unfavourable or severe judgement, comment etc. 2.The analysis or evaluation of a work of art, literature etc.

It is, of course, the second meaning of the word that concerns me here, but the definitions are not mutually exclusive. It is a fact that 'an analysis or evaluation' may come couched in quite damning terms – but serious analysis is worth the bruises. I read an article by a novel writer recently, about his visit to a book market, a *salon litteraire*, in France. He found the punters very blunt in their comments about his work, but concluded: 'Yes, the French revere their novelists, but they also believe they can tell them off if they are found wanting. Because they believe that what you do is important, they also reserve the right to dress you down.'

A bit of dressing down is maybe what we need to make our gardens sing again. Our gardens and our appreciation of them could blossom if we would begin to treat them as important, worthy of serious debate and discussion – not simply as occupational therapy for the retired middle classes.

For the past fifteen years I have been making what I hope is a serious garden – in the sense that I hope it is worth taking seriously, even where it may entertain, amuse or fail. In the absence of any criticism I have had to make my garden in isolation, with no dialogue with my peers. In spite of reading everything I can lay my hands on about gardening, and in spite of visiting every open garden I can get to, I still felt for most of the time that I was working in a void and that this must affect the quality of what I make. So for the past couple of years I have been asking visitors to tell me two things which they believe would improve the garden. This enables people to engage with the subject positively, which I think is easier than saying simply what they think is wrong or not working, and certainly people have been delightfully responsive. Once they get going I often get more than two things to improve my garden, and this can be treasure.

Someone pointed out that a focal point at the end of a walk was being spoilt by a tree just behind it. The trunk was a competing vertical, distracting the eye. This did two things: it made me aware of the problem, which I had been oblivious to; and it gave me the courage to correct it by removing the tree. Someone else pointed out that a fence was obscuring the view of a hornbeam arch, undermining the pleasure of seeing the solid form and shape of the arch. I had never noticed this either until that moment, and it was absolutely right. Of course, the critics have not always been useful (especially when they tell me to get rid of my house). As we lack practice, experience of criticism or a critical vocabulary this is not surprising. I have found even the most sophisticated and experienced visitors often can't see the garden for the plants. The greatest weakness in most people's appraisal appears to be this inability to relate to the whole, a tendency to see a garden as a collection of things. This may arise or be exaggerated by our habit of seeing gardens through the medium of photography.

I also feel sure it is not just criticism of my garden that I need in order to improve my eye. I know that the absence of criticism of other gardens has limited my understanding of design, of the possibilities of expression in a garden. The closest I have come, besides the perpetual, essential dialogue with my husband, has been in some rare and precious discussions with two fellow gardeners, which have raised other fascinating issues. Such as:

Does a splendid colour border in an otherwise indifferent plot make a great garden? If not, why not?

Is an English woodland garden that consists of alien and colourful plants growing under trees simply a horror? If it is (it is), then why? And what would effectively embellish such a wood – sculptural forms to contrast with the bittiness of our native vegetation?

Where and how do weeds affect the aesthetic in a garden?

Is 'good taste' a killer in our gardens? Do we need a bit more honest vulgarity and a willingness to go to extremes in order to revive our tired aesthetic? After all, the gardens that did get taken seriously as art in this country – the landscape gardens of the eighteenth century – were created as ostentatious displays of wealth.

Can a sophisticated person successfully make a deliberately unsophisticated garden? Mary Keen's attempt to do just this in Gloucestershire has odd consequences. She has been committed to making a garden that marries well with the house, an eighteenth-century former rectory with swimming pool. So her concern has been that the garden should be 'unpretentious'. As a result, if it appears rather banal and dull, and the tulips, for example, appear in ill-assorted colours, you find yourself obliged to think that such things are actually deliberate.

What is the ideal relationship between the parts of a garden and the whole? How can a series of rooms work as more than a collection of different bits and become a coherent whole? Can planting be 'meaningless'? Is water a critical component of a garden? Herterton House Garden in Northumberland is a little jewel, but it left me longing for the addition of a reflective water surface to help set off the detailed planting and give rest to the eyes.

Are plants a critical component? What is the role of thought in a garden? How time-sensitive is a garden? Does it need to work all year round, or is one stunning month enough? Is 'stunning' enough?

Do the great gardens of the past still speak to us today? Am I the only person left cold by those huge landscape gardens that demand an endless plod from tree to tree?

To be meaningful, these questions, and many other fascinating questions, have to be discussed in the context of the real gardens that prompted them. Because they were all prompted by actual gardens. And all this – the questions and the reviews – would raise our game and help make excellence worth aiming for. Nothing is more deadly than to have all our gardens described as 'lovely'. If competition is considered by both major political parties to benefit public services, then the competition promoted by intelligent criticism of our gardens would surely provide similar benefits? And we need it, because our gardens are currently blighted by smugness.

I travel the country a lot, interviewing garden owners and writing up their gardens. I have discovered that our gardens sag where they could soar. There is an air of general complacency where I would expect vulnerability. There is a strange lack of eagerness for dialogue. No one asks me my opinion of their garden, what I think are its strengths and weaknesses, or how this or that aspect might be improved. No one says that they have been struggling for months because they know there is something lacking in a particular border, or that they worry that that tree is out of scale and should be removed: what do I think? No one says that they have had this really exciting idea about what to do in a particular place, or that they have decided they will have to change this whole area because it just doesn't work.

If I ask people whether they have any interest in garden criticism they are a bit taken aback. They will say that people would not open their gardens if they thought they would be subject to criticism. Well, tell that to someone who has just had their novel published. Novelists, poets, playwrights: all artists are desperate to be reviewed. It is an indication that the world is taking them seriously and that their work is worth taking seriously. Even the most complacent gardener would want a review if other gardens were getting them. Also people tend to suggest that the whole enterprise is not that important, 'It's just for pleasure' – as if pleasure is easily come by and of little account. And I expect for most people it is, because they appear satisfied with very little aesthetically. These same people will often take the process of gardening terribly earnestly. They go out with salt to torture slugs, double-dig their vegetable plots, go weeding in their nightclothes, or travel hundreds of miles to obtain a plant that doesn't yet feature in the *Plant Finder* – even risk their lives to collect such a plant in the wild. So why do they baulk at taking the resulting garden seriously?

Garden owners also frequently, without apparent embarrassment, tell me that they don't visit other gardens, which I find astonishing. Neither do some garden writers, even more surprisingly. The well known and respected garden writer Robin Lane Fox recently praised the garden Little Sparta in the *Financial Times* (13 December 2003), describing it as 'a vision as elegant as the great 18th century gardeners around Pope and Kent [*sic*] but even wittier and more disturbing.' He then cheerfully admitted: 'I have never seen the results on the ground'.

Perhaps part of the problem is that we describe the backyard where someone has their barbecue, a Capability Brown landscape, which may be commonly regarded as a work of splendid art, and all things in-between, as 'gardens'. Most people have a garden and have to do some gardening. So their association with gardens is more about 'how-to' and plants than art. If someone sits down in front of an easel with a brush in their hand, all their thoughts and cultural notions about art hover over their shoulder, but anyone can happily garden without thinking for a moment about art or aesthetics.

It's astonishing how far into the gardening world this lack of awareness and interest in aesthetics goes. The garden at Barnsley House, near Cirencester, was rather a muddle – a classic case of various bits rather randomly bolted on to one another. The famous vegetable garden was out of scale for human beings, the paths far too narrow and fussy, and the flower borders lacked body and weight. Yet this garden was relentlessly presented as the wonder of the world in Rosemary Verey's lifetime.

And the flip side of this is that when people who have a garden visit a garden of any kind, they know something about it: they understand something of the how-to, even if nothing about design or aesthetics. So know-how tends to be their interest. And most people who visit gardens seem to collect plants, so looking at plants and perhaps obtaining them are often the primary focus of a garden visit.

So there isn't a national outcry about the poor aesthetic standards of the majority of gardens open for charity under the great yellow umbrella of the National Gardens Scheme in England and Wales, because there are nearly always lots of plants to see or plants to buy, and other people's methods of cultivation to compare. It's a kind of hints and tips trip. And, of course, the money goes to charity, and it would hardly be charitable to criticize. The correct attitude towards someone who does a charitable deed is admiration and appreciation, which is what the garden owners get, and like.

And there is no context for garden criticism. The model of theatre or book criticism would suggest that critics would visit gardens, and then write them up in our broadsheet newspapers and periodicals if they were worthy of that attention. But no one writes such a column in this country and no writer has such freedom. Gardens are featured in magazines and newspapers, but never in the review sections. If pop music can be reviewed in these sections, why not gardens?

I had thought that readers of *The Times* would tend to be cultured people, potentially interested in the aesthetics of gardens, so I sent a piece proposing garden criticism to the gardening editor. I received the reply that my article was 'very interesting and does indeed raise some important issues. However, most of our readers seem to want to be inspired and to be shown how to and where to, and judging by recent changes to the RHS "Garden", practical advice is what RHS members want too.'

Gardens usually appear in the press alongside 'home' or 'property', and in glossy magazines which are dedicated to a glamorous presentation, for the benefit of potential advertisers as much as anybody. In both, the 'how to' is muddled up with the resulting gardens – both reduced to hobby. Gardens get into these magazines and the press via photographs. Garden photographers trawl the country looking for new 'material', which they flatter by getting up at the crack of dawn, climbing up ladders, crawling about on the ground and applying filters. They then sell the results to an editor of a magazine or newspaper. The editor then decides whether the photographs fit the magazine – have the right 'style', fill an 'autumn slot', feature the right plants, create the right balance. The editor is merely buying a set of photographs, not assessing a garden. He or she will probably never see the garden. If the photographs are deemed acceptable, a writer will be dispatched to write a piece about the garden. It is not unknown for the writer to compose the piece without setting foot in the garden, but even if they do visit the site, their task is to justify the garden's already accepted presence in the publication, not raise issues about it. Editors ask for the articles to be 'personal, focusing on the owners and their history and how they came to make the garden. With plant associations.' This is altogether not a context in which we can review gardens or discuss them in depth.

We need a context for genuine criticism. We need editors with the courage to break the mould and put gardens alongside books, theatre and pop music in the review sections of our newspapers and magazines. We need to be able to separate garden appreciation from hints on slug control. We need to find a way to break out of the 'gardener's ghetto', where gardens are only seen to be of interest to gardeners. And, perhaps, we need a certain small delinquent boy, prepared to declare that the Emperor in fact has no clothes.

George Carter studied fine art at university, specializing in sculpture. He has worked as a garden designer since 1988 having previously worked as primarily a museum and exhibition designer. His many private gardens in Europe and the United States have ranged in scale from large parks to small town gardens and concentrate on a formal approach to both hard and soft landscaping. His background in exhibition design has led to a theatrical attitude to gardens and he often uses the illusionism of the theatre. He has published widely on different aspects of gardens; his most recent book is *Garden Space* (2005).

Fernando Caruncho is an international landscape designer with over twenty-five years experience. He has designed over 150 private and public gardens in Spain and around the world. His work has been published in *Mirrors of Paradise: The Gardens of Fernando Caruncho* by Guy Cooper and Gordon Taylor (2000).

Charles Chesshire does design and consultancy work in gardens all over Britain. He was director for ten years of Treasures of Tenbury in Worcestershire, the clematis specialists. He is author of three of the RHS Dorling Kindersley Practical Guides: Clematis, Flowering Shrubs and Climbing Plants. His latest book is *Japanese Gardens*.

Gilles Clément studied both agronomy and landscape architecture. Professor at the Ecole du paysage de Versailles since 1979, he has written a dozen books on gardens and ecology while working all over the world. Amongst his most famous creations is a large part of the André Citroën park in Paris. His own remote country garden, La Vallée, remains a constant source of inspiration.

David E. Cooper is professor of philosophy at the University of Durham. He has written widely in the fields of aesthetics and environmental philosophy. His books include *The Measure of Things: Humanism, Humility and Mystery* (2002), *Meaning* (2003), and *A Philosophy of Gardens* (forthcoming, 2006).

Tony Heywood has two distinct horticultural careers. Firstly as a traditional garden designer and director of his garden maintenance and design company and secondly as a horticultural installation artist and leading exponent of the garden as fine art form. His article on the subject, 'Time for a New Garden Style', appeared in the *Garden Design Journal* (March 2004).

Tom Hodgkinson is the editor of the *Idler* (www.idler.co.uk) and author of *How To Be Idle* (2004). He has recently been attempting to grow his own vegetables.

Martin Hoyles is a senior lecturer in communication studies at the University of East London. He has written books on literacy, childhood, mixed-race identity, performance poetry and also several on gardening.

Louisa Jones is an art historian turned writer on and promoter of Mediterranean gardens and cuisine. She lives in Provence. Her forthcoming books include *Provence Harvest* with chef Jacques Chibois (2005) and a joint book with Gilles Clément entitled *Gilles Clément, une écologie humaniste* (2006).

Noël Kingsbury is a designer of gardens and plantings for public spaces, as well as a writer on plants and gardens. He has been particularly active in promoting a scientifically based approach to nature-inspired planting design. His publications include *The New Perennial Garden* (Frances Lincoln, 1996), which was influential in introducing a new concept in naturalistic planting design from continental Europe to an English-speaking audience. He has also co-written two books with Dutch colleague Piet Oudolf.

Lorna McNeur has been a lecturer in architecture at Cambridge University since 1989. She has lectured, published and exhibited her work internationally, most notably at the Guggenheim, Cooper Union, and Art Forum in New York; the AA (and AA Files) in London; and the Fitzwilliam Museum in Cambridge, England. Her forthcoming book is entitled, *Theatre of the City, The Passion for Public Space* (2006).

Rozsika Parker is a psychotherapist and author who gardens. She has published in the fields of art history and psychoanalysis. Her current project, *The Anxious Gardener*, explores the psychological life of the gardener.

Nori Pope and Sandra Pope are responsible for managing one of the most influential gardens in Britain, Hadspen House in Somerset, where the couple work primarily with colour. They have both had a lifetime in practical horticulture.

Tim Richardson is an independent gardens/landscape critic and historian, contributing to several newspapers and magazines. His most recent book is *English Gardens in the 20th Century* (2005); he is also the author of *The Vanguard Gardens and Landscapes of Martha Schwartz* (2004) and *The Garden Book* (2000). He was founding editor of *New Eden* magazine (1998–2000) and was also landscape editor at *Wallpaper* and gardens editor at *Country Life*.

Clare Rishbeth is a lecturer in landscape architecture at the University of Sheffield. She is a published researcher focusing on themes of ethnicity and landscape, addressing the relationship of cultural patterns of perception and use to designed urban spaces.

Anne Wareham is a writer on gardens for a variety of British magazines and newspapers. The garden – Veddw – she has created on the Welsh borders with her husband, Charles Hawes, has been widely written about: it is an example of multiple layers of meaning, commenting particularly on local landscape history.